Kate Walker's
12 Point Guide to Writing Romance

Studymates

25 Key Topics in Business Studies
25 Key Topics in Human Resources
25 Key Topics in Marketing
British History 1870–1918
Business Organisation
The Changing Nature of Warfare 1792–1918
Cultural Studies
English Legal System
English Reformation
European History 1870–1918
European Reformation
Genetics
Getting Started in Radio
Hitler and Nazi Germany (3rd edition)
Land Law
Lenin, Stalin and Communist Russia
Macroeconomics
Organic Chemistry
Poems To Live By
Practical Drama & Theatre Arts
Revolutionary Conflicts
Social Anthropology
Social Statistics
Speaking Better French
Speaking English
Studying Chaucer
Studying History
Studying Literature
Studying Poetry
The Changing Nature of Warfare
The New Science Teacher's Handbook
Troubleshoot Your Problems
Understanding Forces
Understanding Maths
Using Information Technology
War Poets 1914–18
Writing an Academic Essay

Many other titles in preparation

Contents

Introduction

After a long time in writing popular romance fiction (over 16 years) and with over 40 books published, I've learned that the 12 points covered in this book are esssential to creating a novel which grabs the reader and holds them with that vital **PTQ – Page Turning Quality.** They are the elements that appear in every good romance and they remain the same over time, no matter in what decade or even what century the novels are published.

Here are the 12 points in the order I shall be dealing with them.

1. Emotion
2. Conflict
3. Dialogue
4. A sharp focus on hero and heroine
5. Sensuality
6. Passion (and no – passion and sensuality are *not* the same thing!)
7. The hero
8. The heroine
9. Plotting
10. The question 'Why?'
11. The intense Black Moment
12. A believable happy ever after ending

This book is intended as a practical workbook as well as a 'how to write' guide. So each chapter will include some exercises:

1. **Something to read**
   An explanation of one of the 12 points with a discussion of why it's important and how to approach it.

2. **Something to think about**
   Ideas, questions, discussion topics, etc.

3. **Something to do/exercises**
   This is why this book is a *work*book – not just a guide. I want you to do some writing!

Now don't panic. I won't ask for much – you're not going to have to produce a complete 55,000 word novel by the end of this. Most of the exercises will only take no more than a couple of pages or so of writing – 1000 words or less. But if you actually *do* the exercises then hopefully you'll learn more than by just reading the lessons.

What I've found works well when I've taught writing classes, is for people to have a separate notebook or computer file, etc. and make notes as we go along.

▶ Note the topic, and your thoughts on that.

▶ Note the question and write down some ideas and thoughts on that – especially if they surprise you.

▶ Do the exercise – and write down your reactions to it.

Your reactions and thoughts should be as helpful to you as my lessons. You'll learn a lot by looking at your own assumptions, the new ideas that you've come up with as a result of challenging or confirming them, the different ways that you might now think of handling problems as a result of what you've learned. And by the end you'll have a series of notes, ideas and thoughts that you can take further.

Finally, no 'how to' guide can ever actually teach you to write. It's not the case that checking off the points and thinking 'I've done that – and that...' will automatically mean that your submission will be published. What this book does is highlight the areas that, after years of writing and publishing my own novels, working with editors and assessing manuscripts for other writers, I think are important and to give pointers to the way they can be handled successfully. Read through the book, do the exercises, and then try to apply what you've learned to your own work. Hopefully you'll then be able to see where your own personal strengths are and learn more about any weaknesses you have and how to correct them.

1

First Things First

What is a romance?

Before we start, it's vital that we should define exactly what we're trying to write – just what is 'a romance'? This may seem obvious, but this definition is the central core of the sort of novel I write – and that I'm talking about in this book.

If you're interested in writing in the wider ranging field of 'romantic fiction' then this central core still remains the same. But you will need to add in other things – the period details if you are writing a historical novel, the mystery, the thriller plot if you're aiming for suspense, the contemporary setting and references for a 'chick-lit' type of story, the medical background and details if you're writing a medical romance.

So what is a romance?

A romance novel is the story of a man and a woman who, while solving a problem, discover that the love they feel for each other is the sort that comes along only once in a lifetime – leading to a permanent commitment and a happy ending.

Four key elements
▶ A man and a woman (characters).
▶ A problem which threatens to keep them apart (conflict).
▶ A once-in-a-lifetime love.
▶ A permanent commitment and happy ending.

The 'happy ever after ending' is an accepted convention in a romance novel, but it isn't always necessarily a given in all romantic fiction. The same could be said of the once-in-a-lifetime love. In a novel such as the historical saga, particularly one set during war years, there might be the tragic loss of a lover or a husband in the conflict and this could mean an ending without that love in the heroine's life. Equally, under such circumstances, the heroine might find another, second love with whom she faces the future. But the category or 'series' romance usually ends with the hero and heroine committing themselves to each other.

Of course this doesn't necessarily mean that your hero and heroine will be guaranteed to live happily ever after. But this is the point at which the romance novel ends – the point at which your characters have resolved the conflict, overcome the problems that have come between them, and have achieved an equal and mutually supportive partnership in which they can face the future together. What happens after this, or years later, isn't the concern of the current novel, and part of the success of a category romance is that they end on a high point, with all the loose ends tied up, the problems sorted out, leaving the reader feeling satisfied and content as a result.

But the happy ending is part of the reader's expectation of a romance novel. It's one element of the reasons why she picks up a romance instead of any other book. This is the sort of story she's in the mood to read; she knows what to expect from it, and she expects the author to fulfil those expectations. This is one of the main reasons why category or series romance is so successful, selling millions of copies all over the world every year.

Why romance?

Why is romance so hugely successful? It's been estimated that Harlequin romances are sold at the rate of at least six books every minute of every day somewhere in the world. And this company has been achieving this same success rate for a very long time. The original company was founded in 1908 and has been publishing romances ever since. In all that time it has been giving its audience the romantic fantasy that they have been looking for and enjoying, with slight variations according to the decades in which it was published, for almost 100 years.

And this is where we come up against one of the most commonplace and enduring myths about writing romance – the fact that many people believe they are easy to write because they are 'all the same'.

Of course, looking at the rows of similarly packaged books lining the bookshop shelves, all the same size, with the same sort of covers, it is all too easy to believe this is true. But the near-identical packaging does not mean that the contents are exactly the same. The series romance has stood the test of time because it provides the fantasy that the readers want, but it has also adapted to the changes in society, the position of women in that society, the changes in male-female relationships, and the freedom of sexual behaviour so that the books have remained contemporary and up to date too. As a result, it keeps readers coming back again and again for the new titles that are published.

These readers know the authors well. They recognise the individual styles of each writer, the type of story they tell. They know the differences between the lines (see below) too, and they pick and choose according to the mood they're in and the story they want to read.

And this is important because it affects you as a writer.

What type of romance?

Before you can launch into writing a romance, you need to do some preliminary research and spend some time reading and thinking about the genre. As I've already mentioned, romances are not all the same. You need to learn and understand the differences between the lines, decide which ones you personally prefer, and which ones you feel you could write for. The differences may seem slight but they are important. They create the sort of reading experience that the reader wants, and you should be aware of these before you start writing.

For example, just within the lines published by Harlequin Mills & Boon in the UK, you will find the different imprints listed below and more. (I have quoted some of the selling descriptions used for each line to give you some idea of the differences that editors see in them.)

Mills & Boon
Modern Romance
Glamour and sophisticated settings. Seduction and passion.

Tender Romance
Sparkling, fresh and feel-good.

Sensual Romance
Sexy, highly sensual love stories.

Historical Romance
Rich and vivid with their dramatic scope and adventure.

Medical Romance
Exciting, sensual love stories with dedicated caring heroes and heroines.

Blaze
Blaze is full of scorching hot passion, sultry days and steamy nights.

Silhouette
Desire
Intense and passionate.

Special Edition
Strong family themes, compelling, challenging and emotionally satisfying.

Sensation
Exciting, thrilling, dramatic romances where the sexual attractions are undeniable.

Intrigue
Romantic suspense. Thrilling mystery plots entangled with romance.

Red Dress Ink
City girls – 20 to 30-something women who are discovering themselves, sharing apartments, meeting men, struggling with careers and striving for success.

If you want further information or publisher's guidelines on these lines, then more details are available either by writing to Harlequin Mills & Boon (see address in Reference section) or on their website at: *http://www.mills&boon.co.uk*

Which one is for you?

The publisher's guidelines will give you an idea of what the editors are looking for, the length your manuscript should be and where to submit – but if you want to get a real taste for exactly what each line is like and the individual 'flavour' of the books, then you'll need to do some further research for yourself. The best way to do this is to *read*.

Read before you start writing

▶ Read as many different romances as you can get your hands on.
▶ Read examples from all the different lines.
▶ Read as many different authors as you can.
▶ Make notes on what you find out.

You'll need to ask yourself questions as you read:

▶ What sort of heroines do the books feature? Are they independent career girls or quiet, stay-at-home types, or perhaps hardworking doctors in a bustling hospital?

▶ What sort of heroes? Are they sophisticated, wealthy, international men, or 'home-grown' heroes like cowboys, or are they detectives or military men?

▶ How long are the books? For example, the average romance is about 55,000 words, but the historical novels can be up to 90,000.

▶ What point of view is used? Does it stay with one main character only or show both the hero and the heroine's feelings?

▶ Do they have room for a cast of supporting characters or just one or two?

▶ What sort of plots are used – are they passionate, intense and complicated, light-hearted and fun, or are the books thrillers, with mystery and suspense elements?

▶ What is the level of sensuality within each line? Do the books feature vivid, explicit love-making scenes, or are they more restrained, softer focus, more emotional?

▶ Do they require any specific knowledge – like a period in history or the medical practices in a hospital, or military or police procedures that you might have difficulty with?

▶ What other differences or similarities can you find that would influence your liking for this line – and so your writing of it?

Once you have done some basic research like this, you will have a much stronger awareness of the individual approaches of each line and the sort of story editors are looking for. You should also have read across a range of authors and so have come to see the different styles of writing that can appear even within a single line. Then you can start to think about what sort of a romance you can write.

Targeting your romance novel

As you will have seen from your study of the various lines in romance, it's best to try to target your romance to a specific line when you start writing, rather than just writing a story and then trying to make it fit a certain category. Romance writing is a highly competitive market and the editors know exactly what they are looking for, but they are busy professionals who have to deal with thousands of submissions every year. They don't have time to send back detailed criticisms and suggestions for revisions on every manuscript they receive – or even half of them!

So you need to know *before you submit* that you are writing the sort of romance that the editor is looking for in her particular line. Although this sounds obvious, it isn't always the case. Beginners can send the most inappropriate stories to lines where they have no chance at all. Perhaps one of the most common mistakes writers make is to assume that all romances are still the same as they used to be 15 or 20 years ago when their mother read them! They can be in for a shock when they read some of today's output!

If you start writing before you've considered exactly which line you're aiming for, then you could be wasting a lot of time – and possibly setting yourself up for some writer's heartache. You could be writing page after page of interesting, amusing and lively characters only to have the editor tell you she loves the story but all those characters intrude, and would you please cut them out.

Or you could create a powerfully sensual, passionate love scene that the editor says has to go because it's totally inappropriate for the line. Or, perhaps worse, you could just get a form rejection that gives you little or no indication of just what was wrong with your submission.

Careful study of the lines, thinking about what they ask of their writers and targeting your story to fit those needs can help you avoid problems like these, save you time, and the money you would have spent on an inappropriate submission.

Very often, the same story will fit into more than one of the Romance lines published, it is the way that it is written that will fit it into one specific section.

Here are some of the things that you need to consider when targeting your novel to a particular line:

▶ **Emphasis**. How much weight is given to which aspects of the story? So, for example, if you had a highly sensual book that also involved a mystery plot and you were trying to decide whether a book is a Blaze or an Intrigue, then you would need to consider whether the emphasis is on the sexual relationship (Blaze) or solving the mystery (Intrigue).

▶ **Intensity**. Is the conflict between your hero and heroine a harsh, intense, passionate and possibly even dangerous one, or is it more emotional, less abrasive, as your characters overcome the barriers between them and find true happiness in the romance of a lifetime?

▶ **Characters**. In some of the lines – Modern Romance is one example – many other characters would diffuse the intensity. In a Special Edition, with its emphasis on family themes, more characters would be an asset.

▶ **Sex**. It's not just that in one line it's not allowed and in another it is, or that it's more frequent in some lines than others. You can have a book where there is just one major passionate scene but it falls into one line because of the intensity of the rest of the relationship. Or one where they make love openly and clearly on the page but because the atmosphere is very different it is a gentler Tender Romance.

▶ **Conflict**. This is a major point in deciding which line you're aiming for. If you want to write strong, meaty stories, then you will aim for a line that has greater scope for a stronger conflict. (But make sure you don't confuse 'conflict' with 'argument' – we will come back to this later in the section on conflict.)

▶ **Subplots**. Does the line have room and a large enough word count for them or not? Once again it's the *emphasis* that makes the difference.

▶ **Enjoyment**. In the end it comes down to the question of which line you personally enjoy reading most; the line that you can relate to, that excites and interests you and whose characters you find most appealing. If you detest the Alpha male type of hero in some of the books (Modern is the most typical example of this) then you are not likely to be able to create such a hero without turning him into a totally unsympathetic monster that no woman could love.

Perhaps enjoyment is one of the most important reasons for writing romance – any kind of romance. A lot of people have the impression that writing romance is so simple, that the books can just be dashed off – or 'churned out' – and then because they sell well that they are a quick and easy way to make a lot of money. The problem is that because romance novels are so easy to read, there is the assumption that this makes them just as effortless to write.

And this brings me to the problem of the romance *formula*.

The 'formula' for writing romance novels

Whenever people find out that I write romance – and especially when they discover that I write for Harlequin Mills & Boon – there is always someone who comments about that fact that the books are all written to a 'formula'. They tell me that all you have to do is to discover how that formula works and you can churn out endless bestsellers, make a fortune and retire to a tax haven for the rest of your life. I wish!

I've even met people who believe that I operate 'the computer'. They are convinced that there is a computer somewhere which has endless variations on the romance theme filed away inside it – plots, settings, twists – everything. All you have to do is to choose a name for your hero and heroine, decide on a nationality – Greek Tycoon, Spanish Billionaire, American Cowboy, program that in and press the right button. The computer whirrs and clicks and spews out a perfectly formed novel with those characters at the centre of it. This way, one person alone writes *all* the Harlequin Mills & Boon novels, every single month, using an endless variety of pen names to disguise the fact!

These stories always stem from someone who has never read a romance and knows nothing about the publishing industry at all. The formula has become one of the most popular urban myths in existence – along with the story of the 'authors' instruction book'. This is supposed to be handed to every author who writes for Mills & Boon and it is said to detail exactly what heroes and heroines we are allowed to write, giving body types and colourings, ages and nationalities. It is also supposed to detail exactly what type of physical contact is allowed and what is forbidden – parts of the body that may be touched – by whom and in what situations! Well, I've been writing for Mills & Boon since 1984, and neither I nor any of my fellow authors have ever seen this famous book – it's another urban myth.

As the RITA prizewinning Mills & Boon and Silhouette novelist Anne McAllister said to me, very wisely, the romance 'formula' is only a framework in the same way that the poetic form of sonnet is a framework, within which you can write anything you want and work in any way you want.

The formula is a creation of fantasy, something that has never existed – but there could be said to be a basic format for writing a romance – a framework around which all the books are built. This is so very simple that anyone who thought about it for a moment could probably come up with something close. Whenever I teach workshops or classes, this is the 'formula' that I give out.

The Formula

Heroine

+

Hero

+

Conflict

+

'Getting to know you'

+

Lowest point (the Black Moment)

+

Resolution

+

Happy ending

= Romance

Writing from the heart

There isn't a formula to writing romance – there isn't even a detailed instruction book to tell you exactly how to go about it. But people still want to believe that some sort of formula exists. They long to know the 'secret' to writing romances that an editor will buy and publish and that readers will buy, read, and come back looking for more.

And there is an important secret to this sort of writing that, while it can't guarantee any sort of success, will give you a far better chance of creating a romance that an editor will be interested in reading.

What is this secret? It can be summed up in four short words.

Write from the heart.

It's no coincidence that many of the most successful romance writers were also – and still are – ardent romance readers themselves. The people who love reading romance value it for the special sort of writing it is and they appreciate the stories as the emotional reads they are. And as a result they can write successful novels because they write them from the heart.

Over the years many people have tried to write romance because it's 'easy' or because they believe they can make a fortune quickly by doing so. They approach their writing with a degree of cynicism, or laughingly imitate what they believe a romance should be. These books fail because the lack of respect in the author's mind shows in the writing.

To write romance successfully, you need to immerse yourself in the world of the books, you have to get inside your characters' skins, feel the emotions they are experiencing, and communicate that emotion to your readers. You need to have your own individual voice that marks your books out from all the others, not just turn in some pale copy of an author who has gone before. And you need to care about the people whose story you are telling, and want to show that in your story.

It is almost impossible to create any truly original plot for a romance. Every plot or theme that is appropriate to this genre has probably been used, often many times over. Some of them are so tried and true that they have names of their own like 'The Secret Baby Plot' or 'Marriage of Convenience'. We will look at some of these later when we discuss plotting and the 'hooks' that catch a reader's interest. But you can have all the hooks in the world in your story and if you don't truly care about the people involved in it then your story will not have any heart. And it is that 'heart' that makes a reader enjoy your story from start to finish. It's the 'heart' that makes her want to read more so that she'll pick up your next book in the shops – and the next – because she sees *your* name on it.

The format that I have quoted here is just the most basic, minimal skeleton of a story that forms the framework of any romance novel. After that, it's the details, the insights, the personalities, the backgrounds, that you as the author create which flesh out that skeleton until it forms a living, exciting, intriguing story that makes a successful romance novel.

And how do you do that?

I will give you some ideas and suggestions as you work through the 12 points of this book.

12 questions about reading romance

1. Is the book a contemporary romance, historical or medical? If it is contemporary, which line does it appear in – Modern (Presents), Tender (Romance), Sensual, Blaze, etc?

2. What sort of heroine does the book have? Does she seem appropriate to the period and setting?

3. What sort of hero does the book have? Is he a powerful, Alpha male or something different?

4. How long is the book? How are the chapters or sections divided?

5. What point of view is used? Does it change frequently or not at all?

6. How many characters are there? Does the book have room for supporting characters?

7. Are there similarities in the development of the plots in a number of books you have read – in the number and placement of complications, tension, love scenes, etc?

8. How much sensuality is there in the book – is it a passionate, sensual story or more restrained?

9. How does the author get the reader involved at the beginning of the story?

10. How is each character presented to the reader? When does the heroine first appear? When does the hero first appear?

11. How does the author make you care about the characters?

12. How much did you enjoy this book – as a reader – and as a potential writer? Is this the sort of romance you feel you could write?

2

Emotion

We're looking at ways to put that all-important *heart* into your romance – and the first, and most important way to do this is **emotion**.

Why is emotion so important?

Direct quote 1:
Question to an editor from Harlequin Mills & Boon:

'What three things are most important in making a book a best seller?'

Editor's answer:

'Emotion, emotion, emotion.'

Direct quote 2
'Think of the emotion that you believe your scene needs – and then double it.'
Emma Darcy (bestselling romance writer)

Your reader picks a romance – and specifically a Harlequin Mills & Boon romance – because she wants an *emotional* read. If she wanted a satire on society in England in the Regency period, she'd choose Jane Austen. If she wanted a deep, complex and ambiguous historical novel, then she will look for an author like Dorothy Dunnett. If she wanted a dark crime thriller, she'd pick up – well – insert your own favourite crime author's name here.

Giving the reader what they want

From the start your reader wants to enjoy and experience the emotions of your heroine – and probably your hero too – along with them. She wants to experience the tug of attraction that reaches out to both the main characters from the moment they first meet. She wants to identify with the heroine and fall in love with the hero – and she wants to live through all the feelings they have along the way towards the happy ending that she knows is coming up.

We're talking about reader expectation here. The reader knows when she picks up a romance that the happy ending is guaranteed, so she's not reading the book to find out *what* happens – she knows what that's going to be – it will follow the pattern of the format – the skeleton I quoted in the last chapter. There will be a meeting, an irresistible attraction, but a conflict will drive the hero and heroine apart. She knows that the conflict will be resolved – that's not the question. What she wants to know, and enjoy is *how* that happens, and to do this she has to live through the experience along with the characters.

So your reader wants to feel the same anger that your heroine feels when she thinks the hero has betrayed her, she wants to know the anger, the hatred that results from that betrayal. She hopes to be caught up in the tensions, the conflict that come between them. The whole experience of reading the book should send her on the same emotional roller-coaster ride that the characters go through, going up and down, through happiness and hope, to bitterness and despair. At the point that is known as the 'Black Moment', when everything seems to be lost and it looks as if the happiness that your characters yearn for and that your reader dreams of for them, she wants to feel their fear, to actually doubt, just for the moment, that the happy ending is actually possible even though she knows it will happen. And she wants to know the intense relief, the sense of delight, when everything is finally resolved and the tension melts into a feeling of happiness and completion.

It's this emotional experience that a reader is looking for. It's the reason why she's picked up a romance in the first place. If that's what your book provides, she'll enjoy it and look for your name on a cover again. And if you short-change her she won't be best pleased, and she'll be very unlikely to come back for more.

Very often these days, emotion is scorned or openly despised. Books that are cold, precise, analytical and controlled, are often favoured over big, sprawling, emotional reads. And yet we talk of the 'greats' – Dickens, the Brontës – *Jane Eyre* – *Gone with the Wind* – with such delight because the emotions in them are memorable.

You need to look at your writing and think about how emotional it is – in style, in characters, in subject, in conflict, in pace – and see if you can take it up a degree or two – or more – without it going right over the top.

We're not talking about purple prose here. Just emotional writing. Writing that tugs at the heart, makes it beat a little faster. Tangles up your feelings, gets you totally absorbed in what's happening. Above all, writing and situations that make you *care* about what happens to the characters in the story.

The emotional tension is vital. The reader wants to become deeply involved with your characters, to really care for them, and to feel that they are risking real pain, real loss, real heartache in the relationship they are involved in.

Emotional punch

Many people submit their manuscript to Harlequin Mills & Boon and get it back with the comment that it 'lacks the emotional punch that is vital for this particular line'. They may also be told that 'it fails to reach an emotional climax'. The slightly sexual references are not accidental. The reading of a romance should come across like a good (preferably great) sexual experience – building up from interest to arousal to passion to that 'emotional climax'. We've all been there. We've all galloped our way through a great book, knowing we just can't put it down, needing to read more and more and more – but at the same time knowing we don't want it to end. And then we get to the 'climax' and we sigh our delight and satisfaction – and wish it wasn't over.

To achieve this, you need to get your reader *involved* with your characters and their situation and problems. Over the course of a story, the problems they face should grow worse, larger, harder to handle or apparently insoluble. The emotional effect on the characters should grow deeper as the problems worsen, and the involvement of the reader grows right along with the difficulties the characters face. The movement of the books should be like a series of zigzags, or Ws – with emotion going up and down – two steps forward – and one step back. It should go through tension to a painful pitch, then ease off a little – maybe even seeming to have everything going right – only to introduce some new complication that destroys the fragile peace.

What is emotional punch?

As we've seen, emotional punch is created by the feeling of emotional involvement, empathy and absorption that a reader feels when caught up in the story. It is he emotional rapport she feels with the characters and the steadily growing pace of the story and the emotional development that gives it its PTQ (Page Turning Quality). When a reader is deeply involved in the story and cares about the outcome then, as she is reading, she will turn the pages more and more quickly because she wants to know what will happen and how it will happen. She won't want to put the book down, and if she has to then she will want to pick it up again as soon as possible.

Emotional punch is easy to recognise when you're reading. It's more difficult to understand when you're writing and to know how to put it into a book when an editor has said that it's lacking that vital oomph.

So perhaps it's better to start off with some ideas of what emotional punch is *not*.

What emotional punch is not

It's not just conflict, arguing or shouting
We will look at conflict in much more detail later on, when we discuss what sort of conflict works in a romance. But for now, the sort of conflict I mean is just plain bad tempered, constant arguing, with the hero and heroine shouting at each other, throwing out accusations and calling each other names. I read many manuscripts by beginners who are aiming their work at the romance market, only to find that the hero and heroine are constantly nasty to each other, often downright abusive, for no or very little reason.

There is an impression that a romance consists of the two central characters disliking each other on sight and then proceeding to argue, snipe and generally be unpleasant until the last chapter when they declare their love for each other. This couldn't be further from the truth.

If your hero and heroine are in conflict over something, it should be over something that really matters. Something that they feel strongly or care strongly about for very good reasons. With this sort of conflict, then it is perfectly possible for the couple to be consistently polite, even affectionate towards each other and yet be miles apart emotionally.

The effect of a constant, unrelenting nastiness and accusations is twofold:

1. It has the feeling of being in a room with two strangers who are conducting an argument that really should be held in private. The observer feels uncomfortable, out of place, wishing they were anywhere but there. It is not the same feeling at all as being with two people you care about, and whose disagreement you can understand on both sides, so that you wish desperately you could help while feeling there is nothing that you can do to change their minds.

2. If the disagreement is always on the same topic, the arguments becoming circular and never changing, the mood never varying, then there is no room at all for character growth or change and the effect is that of a constant, infuriating noise that you just wish you could switch off. No one is going to believe that these two people really do love each other at the end. The reader needs variations of mood and atmosphere, to see different sides of each character in order to come to care for them, and to want them to come together happily at the end.

To quote one of my personal favourite Modern/Presents authors – Anne McAllister:

> '*Presents* is always about strong emotion. That is not to be confused with dysfunction. Characters can operate out of deep emotional reservoirs and not be arrogant and bullying or shrill and weepy, or basically so obnoxious that in real life we would not want to be anywhere near them. My favourite characters in *Presents* are the ones who feel deeply about things – who are passionate about their beliefs, but who are people I would genuinely want to know.'

It's not endless crying, bewailing or self pity
Emotional tension does not result from the heroine feeling miserable all the way through the book and weeping or moaning to herself, her family and friends because the hero doesn't love her. Especially in the contemporary romance (Tender and Modern, etc) the heroine is far more likely to have to get on with her life and her job. Collapsing into a self-pitying heap, drowning in an ocean of tears, is far more likely to make the reader want to shake her and wish that she would grow up – fast!

Her heart – or his – may be breaking, but there is more emotional tension to be created in a scene in which she or he pretends that they don't care at all, that nothing matters and they are perfectly fine. The contrast between the truth and the mask they wear is much more effective in tugging at the reader than endless weeping and wailing.

It's not just the heroine being cruelly treated and enduring for love
The heroine is the reader's 'filter' into the story. The action and events are usually seen through her eyes and the reader wants to empathise with her and feel the emotions she is going through. But piling misery on misery, or having the hero behave in the most appalling manner to her and having her put up with that because she loves him, is not the way to create an emotional response in the reader and an emotional punch to the story.

If the heroine goes through every torment possible – being lied to, condescended to, seeing the man she loves with another woman, being used sexually and then abandoned, threatened with bankruptcy – and any other horror you can think of, then the reader will end up punch-drunk from all the blows. And the cumulative effect will make your heroine into a victim your reader can't respect and your 'hero' into a man no sane person could love.

It is not manipulative
In the same way, giving your heroine every trauma in the book – the loss of her parents in a car crash, a broken relationship, perhaps an abusive lover, a stillborn baby or a miscarriage, terrible financial difficulties in her past – is not the way to get sympathy for her and add to the emotional impact of her story. Why is this? The answer is again in the reasons why the reader wants to enjoy a romance.

What a reader wants from a romance is to become absorbed in the developing relationship between the hero and the heroine as it is happening in the present in the book. The past and its traumas may have an effect on that relationship, but it is how the characters deal with the effect of those traumas that matters. That is the sort of emotion that the reader is looking for, and particularly the way that they move on from them, putting the scars of old wounds behind them so that they can learn to love and live again. That is where the emotion should be centred, not in the past.

So if there is a trauma in the past it should be there for a very good reason. It affects the present, has to be dealt with – and by showing the hero and heroine dealing with it in the present you move their relationship on several stages, changing the balance in it and working it into a new form that can take them into the future. To quote Mills & Boon Modern Romance author Anne McAllister: 'You can't just put in a dead baby in order to up the emotion quotient and make people cry.'

It's not just using words like 'angrily', 'sarcastically', 'fearfully or 'miserably'
The constant use of adverbs like these, particularly at the end of a speech, such as

'he said angrily', 'she replied sarcastically', has little or no effect if the words that precede them don't fit with the description. It is far more effective to make your characters actually speak words that *sound* sarcastic, angry, cold, etc. That gets across their character, their mood or the atmosphere in the room in a far more dramatic and immediate way than simply describing them.

One of the most frequently quoted rules for effective popular writing is 'show don't tell' and here is an important case in point. If you *show* the mood and the emotion in the dialogue, using words that can only be angry or cynical or whatever, it will have much more immediacy and drama and so much more emotional punch than any way of *telling* your reader how it was said. If you read the words aloud and they have a natural tone of voice that goes with them, then you know you've succeeded and you don't need to add 'coldly', 'cynically', 'brutally' or any other adverb to get across how they are used.

It is not just sentiment

A vital part of a developing romance is what is termed 'getting to know you time'. This is when your central characters learn more about each other and as they learn, they discover parts of each other's characters that they never expected to find. In a relationship where there has been a lot of conflict or a lot of disagreements, when the hero and heroine have constantly found themselves on opposing sides, then this 'getting to know you time' often involves discovering softer, gentler sides of their personalities.

But these discoveries shouldn't be made in sentimental ways. For example, a hero's softer side isn't best displayed by him rescuing abandoned puppies or kittens or sending sickly love letters just in order to create the 'Aaah!' factor. You need to delve deeper into your hero's (or heroine's) character and find something that will come right from their heart, something that is intensely personal to them and that will mean all the more, perhaps because they have to struggle to reveal it as it is so private and intimate.

It is not cliché

In much the same way, the emotion in a story is not shown to its best advantage in the traditional, tried and true 'hearts and flowers' way.

Whenever people think of romance, they tend to think in terms of a dozen red roses or a huge box of chocolates. But for every woman who loves roses, there will be a dozen who prefer other flowers altogether. And for some women, perhaps someone who is trying to watch her weight, that box of chocolates will not be any sort of gift, but a burden and a temptation they don't want.

True 'romance' comes from really understanding the character of the person you care about and acting or choosing gifts accordingly. And in any romance story, the emotional punch comes not from the often repeated, over used, clichéd scenes. It is the sudden, unexpected action, the thoughtfulness that cares for the person as they really are, that has a greater impact in the emotional punch stakes.

It is not just manipulating events into things that 'always happen in a romance'
This is another form of cliché. The sort of event I'm talking about is the tired, overused scenario – like the moment when the heroine sees the hero in a restaurant with another woman and believes he is unfaithful to her – or vice versa. Or when the heroine falls down the stairs and miscarries so that her hero realises how much he loves her. As I've already said, it's much more important to bring out the characters of your hero and heroine, and make the tensions and the problems flow from there, rather than bringing out scenes that you have read in other romances.

Why is emotional punch so important?

We've already acknowledged that romance readers are looking for the **development** of the emotional relationship between your hero and heroine. They might want the addition of suspense, comedy, history, medical details – but this is the central vital element. Emotional punch can also add to your writing in other ways:

▶ **Pace** – the gathering emotional 'snowball'/floodtide getting bigger and bigger and faster and faster as it thunders on its way until it's beyond control and sweeps everything before it.

▶ **Reader identification** – so that they are involved in the lives of the characters and *care* about what happens, so they don't want to put the book down.

▶ **Page turning quality** – that keeps the reader going on and on and on until they reach the end.

▶ **Satisfaction** – that 'AAAAH' feeling at the last page – or just sitting quietly remembering.

▶ **Memorability** – they will remember that one where he gave her the necklace of leaves he had collected for her (*Constantine's Revenge*). Or when he had the contents of the room in which he was going to propose packed up and taken to Sicily, waiting for a chance to propose again (*The Sicilian's Wife*). As a result, they will remember the author's name and want more of her books.

How to achieve emotional punch

Create characters you care about
We will discuss creating characters in more detail later, but you need to create characters who will grab at the reader's emotions and make them care. To do this you need characters who come alive on the page. So you need to create:

▶ Characters who have pasts/relationships/experiences/lives before your story starts.

▶ Characters who don't just appear on the first page.

▶ Characters the reader can find sympathetic.

▶ Characters who have believable emotions – emotions that spring from the characters they are – not imposed on them from outside. These emotions drive the story, they are not created by the author in order to fit in with the direction she wants the story to turn.

The hero may be more inhibited about telling his feelings – but this can be even more 'emotional' as he struggles to find the right words.

The heroine is usually more open about her feelings but her life experiences might make her scared/nervous/distrustful and so unwilling to show them.

But you as the writer need to know what your characters are feeling inside and to show *why* they behave as they do.

▶ Understand your characters' motivations and mine them deeply.

Action and reaction – character before plot

Remember why readers are reading a romance – for that emotional journey. So you need to make your plot flow from the behaviour and personalities of your central characters. The hero or the heroine behaves in a certain way and then the other one reacts to that behaviour, creating a development in the plot, rather than a series of particular events imposed on the characters from outside by the author.

The more complicated a plot in events, the more risk there is of losing the emotional theme that is running through the book. If you have mysteries that have to be solved, events that have to happen, secondary characters whose experiences have to be sorted out, then these can force the plot in directions that impose restrictions on your central characters. Your hero and heroine and their relationship should always be central to everything and more important than any other details.

You need to concentrate on the emotion and bring that out first. Then shade in the rest of the plot.

A real love

Because you have to concentrate on this central relationship, you need to make sure that what you are describing is a very special, deep and heartfelt sort of emotion. Remember the definition of a romance – this should be a once-in-a-lifetime sort of love, and that is how it should come across to your reader.

The relationship between your hero and heroine should have real depth, real value. They should not appear to be just a passing fancy, not just a crush. They should be someone of real value to each other, someone who they would want to spend a life with. Someone who will make every day brighter and better if they win through and start a life together.

This is important because if the relationship has such a deep, valuable meaning then it will automatically raise the emotional stakes in your story. Now there is something of real value that someone can lose. Something that will make their life feel empty and hollow if it isn't there. So, this relationship is something that your characters will want to fight for and your reader will be cheering them on, wanting them to succeed.

Time for reflection
Without reflection your plot can become like a runaway train, or hammer blows to the head that just won't stop. It is just a series of events, with no indication of how these events and the emotional implications of them are affecting the characters whose emotional story you are telling. Your characters need to:

▶ react to what's happening
▶ vent their feelings
▶ change and develop
▶ decide what to do next.

It is these insights into your characters' inner thoughts that will make your reader feel they are getting to know them personally. This is especially the case when the characters' thoughts reveal secrets to the reader that they are not prepared to show to the other characters in the story. As a result, the reader feels as if they are really involved with this person's feelings and thoughts.

Knowing your hero and heroine's thoughts will also help your reader connect and sympathise with them. This is particularly so when any one of your characters is doing something that could seem cruel, thoughtless or unkind. When the reader is let into their thoughts they will understand the character's reasoning, however faulty, and will not be alienated as a result. Instead they will understand, and relate to the character involved.

Reflection/introspection shows the characters' emotional development and this is a vital part of the journey that the reader makes through the book. They want to see how your hero and heroine move from perhaps detesting each other wholeheartedly at the start, through mistrust, doubt, uncertainty to wondering, understanding, liking and eventually to that deep and meaningful love that will enable them to commit to each other for the future. In the past, particularly for the hero, his point of view was rarely shown and so it could appear that he had been foul and unpleasant all the way through the story, only to suddenly announce that he was in love with the heroine in the last chapter. Now it is possible to show the hero's feelings, thoughts and emotional development, as well as the heroine's, and readers have said that they enjoy this extra aspect of the internal reflection in a book. We will come back to this in Chapter 5 when we discuss point of view.

Another role that introspection serves is to give the reader time to 'take a breather' from the punches of emotion so that they don't end up punch-drunk with all that is happening. Just as in real life, when emotion needs to be recollected in tranquillity in order to absorb it and adjust to it, so the reader also needs to have some time away from the emotional and dramatic scenes in the book to reflect on what has been happening and decide how they feel about it.

'Getting to know you'

Another vital part of creating 'emotional punch' is in the sections of the book that are labelled the 'getting to know you' time. These are the stages in the story where the hero and heroine have a chance to spend quieter time together, to talk about more ordinary things, to learn about each other's lives and pasts and families. And by learning about these things, they also learn and come to understand just why certain things are flashpoints to each other; why the other reacts so strongly to certain triggers.

This is important as a balance to the heated arguments, the dramatic confrontations, the conflict and tension that keep the hero and heroine apart. No matter how far apart they might have seemed at the beginning of the story, if the book is to have a believable happy ending, then at some point they are going to have to come close together, to fall deeply and lastingly in love, and head off into the future together. The initial impact, the first wild falling headlong into love might have happened very quickly, but the reader needs to have some evidence that their relationship has deeper roots than this. How can it be the love of a lifetime if they never learn about each other? The 'getting to know you' times will add in this important stage.

The other important aspect of this time is that it can show other, more relaxed, gentler sides to your characters' personalities. These are times when they can reminisce, discuss, joke, tease. It is possible to have fun, to laugh, even in the middle of the worst dramas, and by showing these lighter moments you will add to the reader's identification with your characters, so making them care more about them – all of which will increase the emotional impact of their story. After a period of calm, of lighter mood in which your hero and heroine seem to be coming closer and gaining an understanding of each other, tearing them apart with some new crisis will have much more impact as a result.

Dialogue

I've already discussed the use of dialogue, and its all-important effect on the 'show don't tell' rule earlier, and we'll come back to it again when we deal with dialogue in detail in Chapter 4. Dialogue is one of the best possible ways of adding to the emotional punch of a story. Use it well; use it often. But always remember these points:

▶ Make it sound real and appropriate to the character who is speaking.

▶ Make it sound emotional.

▶ Make it sound angry, sad, sarcastic or loving – don't just describe it that way.

Nothing makes the scene more dramatic than powerful, appropriate dialogue well used so that it makes the reader feel they really are there. But at the same time, nothing is more likely to pull the reader out of a story and so kill any emotional punch than dialogue that doesn't fit with the character or where the reader is just told that it's cynical or sarcastic or bitter or cruel but they never actually 'hear' it themselves.

Show don't tell
Again I must emphasise that showing the reader a scene developing before her eyes, with action and dialogue, not just telling her about it, adds to the drama of your story. It quickens the vital pace of a scene, and makes it much more vivid and alive. As well as dialogue, other important ways of getting across the mood and drama of the scene you are describing are by using:

▶ Body language.

▶ Actions and their pace – fast and jerky, angry, slow, lazily indolent – all these bring the scene alive.

▶ They also make sure that your characters are not just talking heads – we will come back to this again when dealing with dialogue in more detail.

Reading between the lines – subtext
The subtext beneath the conversation can be an important tool in building up the emotional tension of a scene, especially if you are using it to contrast what is appearing on the surface – and what the other character(s) can see or hear and what is really going on in the character's head.
    So you would be able to contrast:

▶ What they're saying with what they're really thinking.

▶ What they're doing with why they're really doing it.

▶ What they believe with how they're pretending to act.

► Something they know that the reader can be let in on while the other person/people in the room are left out.

► This can be emphasised by using the viewpoint of the character whose thoughts are in opposition to their actions. We will cover viewpoint in more detail later.

High drama

As stated above, it is important to make the conflict something worth fighting over. This is especially important if you are creating scenes of high drama where huge emotional upheavals are involved. Big emotion has to be justified or it will just seem melodramatic.

► If you want your characters to react strongly you have to create conflicts that warrant fighting over and behaving in cruel, potentially dangerous and destructive ways. The hero particularly cannot behave like a monster, simply because 'that's what romance heroes are like'.

► Make sure that your characterisation is strong – create characters who would react in strong passionate ways to the situations they find themselves in.

► Difficult choices – give your characters problems that are hard to deal with; problems that make the characters struggle to cope. A simple, straightforward choice means that there is a simple, straightforward answer. But if your characters have complex moral decisions to make, or are in situations where their head wars with their heart, where what they feel contradicts what they have been told, then their struggle to find an answer will pull the reader in and make them empathise with their problems.

► Raise the stakes – just when it looks as if all is going well – put in something new or something they had forgotten about that still holds them back.

Powerful prose

► Use language vividly when you are writing, especially in emotional scenes. Use symbols and metaphors to enhance your descriptions and bring the picture home to your reader.

► Use details of the scene – the way your hero looks, your heroine's scent, sensual materials of the clothes or the furnishings. Employ all the five senses to add to the atmosphere.

▶ Describe the way your characters are feeling and don't be afraid to echo it in their thoughts – neat and tidy thoughts are not emotional ones, but broken, disjointed, angry and unfinished sentences communicate mood much more accurately.

▶ Use the most dynamic verbs you can think of and build them up to add to the emotion and drama in a scene:
   – he strode/marched instead of 'walked'
   – she screamed/yelled/whispered – not 'she said'
   – he thumped/beat/banged on the door – not 'knocked'.

Use environment

▶ Use the environment and the setting that they're in to reflect/contrast/ illuminate their feelings.

▶ Think about the different ways that different settings will affect how they are feeling. A deeply luxurious house will contrast sharply with a misery of heart, and perfect accord and happiness can make a shabby, uncomfortable room into a wonderful place.

▶ What about the weather? How can you use that to add to the misery or increase the tension? A snowstorm outside can prevent the characters from ever getting away from each other and trap them together, no matter what they feel about each other. If you keep your characters in close proximity then the tensions between them will grow – when they can't get away from each other they have to deal with things. In a less confined environment, they could walk away and you have to get them back together, but the tensions of confinement are very different. A threatening thunderstorm will make the atmosphere feel even more oppressive and the moment that the storm breaks can be used to great effect when it breaks into the dialogue or shatters a sudden silence.

Or what about the way that a flash of lightning can light up a previously darkened room? What would your characters see?

Intense heat or bitter biting cold will draw very different reactions from your hero and heroine – how will they cope – and of course there is always the question of what they will do to warm up!

If one of your characters is outside, perhaps trying to find help then pouring rain will add to the misery. Or equally, getting soaked through to the skin can be fun – with the right person.

Good diversions

If you watch TV soap operas you will see how diversions and distractions can be used to increase the tension and add drama to a scene. The same can be done in a romance.

But try to avoid clichéd interruptions – the most obvious one is the telephone ringing just when the couple are about to make love. If you can think of something else it will give your story a fresher feel.

And if you do want your heroine to say no to the hero, then show the reasons why she's doing so. In a modern romance it can be harder to find a reason why she will say no than it used to be to let her say yes! In a historical novel it is far more likely that the heroine will be afraid of ruining her reputation but if you are writing a *contemporary* romance then you will need something that might really happen and not just a sudden change of mind.

Foreshadowing

If you give your reader information that other characters don't know, then an added tension will come from the fact that the reader can see something coming. So when a scene shows something happening between your hero and heroine, or when it happens to other people, the reader can see that it will fit in later in a different way. Or a mini argument that will later be major confrontation.

The most obvious example of this is the 'Secret Baby' plot, when the heroine has the hero's child hidden away upstairs, or at a friend's house. The hero doesn't even know of the child's existence, but the heroine's thoughts will be constantly turning to the child and the secret she is keeping. The reader is also in on the secret and is waiting for the inevitable moment when the hero must find out.

Black Moment/Grey Moment

One particular way of foreshadowing is to use the Grey Moment to lead up to the Black Moment. The Grey Moment is when the couple confront some important issue that seems like the main crisis – it is disturbing but not shattering. It knocks them down and leaves them vulnerable, but they manage to deal with it and then seem to have reached a sort of peace.

But if you have set your scene up well, then the reader will know that the real knockout blow is still coming. There is something that they haven't dealt with and it's about to explode right in their faces. And because of this temporary truce and peace, it will have much more emotional impact.

Mystery

Any mystery that needs solving will always keep people reading. They want to know the answer:

- ▶ What happened?
- ▶ Why did this happen?
- ▶ How did it happen?
- ▶ Who is he?
- ▶ Why did she do that?
- ▶ Who is the baby's father?

If you set up a mystery and thread clues to the answer all through the book then you will give your story that PTQ because the reader wants to know the answers.

Passion/sex

This will of course need separate sections of its own – but it is an important element in the emotional punch of a story.

Sexual tension will always create emotional punch – but the important word here is 'tension'. Remember it is the anticipation, the build up, that creates the tension, and that can be there in a look, a smile, a word, a glance.

You need to build up a sense of inevitability, a powerful feeling that this is the unstoppable force between the two characters. It is not the act itself that has the punch – that can create a sense of anticlimax when it's over. It is the rising tide of passion that builds the tension you want.

Hooks

There is a great saying about never ending a chapter with your heroine drifting off to sleep unless you want the reader to do that too! If you end your chapter on an exciting moment then the reader will want to continue to find out just what is going to happen.

Similarly if you start the next chapter with some intriguing piece of dialogue or exciting event, then she will want to carry on reading as soon as she sees it.

Honesty

Finally, what you need to remember is that the most important factor in creating emotional intensity is the author's willingness to delve into her own strong emotions. To write about a character's emotions, you must be able to feel those emotions. If your character falls in love, then you have to feel it. If she is rejected by the hero then you need to remember a time when you were rejected. It hurt. Let yourself experience that emotion again. Now use that knowledge and feeling to write about how your character feels. You will know what thoughts go with the feeling, how someone who's feeling that hurt will act, what they'll say. Reliving your own strong emotions can be difficult, but it's an important part of developing power in your writing.

You need to be honest with your own emotions rather than create a construct – writing in the 'emotion' as a secondary aim, an attainable skill can never fully work. There will be a gap between real feelings and the feeling you *think* you should create and that will end up in the words on the page.

After all, people don't show their deepest emotions easily – it's that struggle that makes it emotional. You have to feel that struggle, go through it with them and then write the emotion as honestly as you can.

You have to write from the heart – that is what will give your story the heart it needs.

12 questions about emotional punch

1. Have I allowed time for my characters to explore their feelings?

2. Have I made sure that the plot doesn't get in the way of the characters' emotions?

3. Have I shown emotions through dialogue, body language, the choices my characters make?

4. Have I hinted at a subtext – thoughts and feelings below the surface?

5. Have I allowed my characters to react with emotions true to their personalities?

6. Have I used specific details to create a picture so vivid that my reader reacts emotionally?

7. Have I created a conflict worth being divided over?

8. Have I put my characters into the most dramatic situations possible – remembering to justify the emotions this creates?

9. Have I raised the stakes to force my characters to make tough decisions?

10. Have I use dynamic verbs and adjectives?

11. Have I used the environment to reflect, contrast with or illuminate my characters' emotions?

12. Do I feel emotion when I read the most dramatic scenes in my book?

Exercises

Something to think about

Think back over books you've read in the past – the ones you've most enjoyed – the ones that made your heart beat faster or made tears sting your eyes – or even made you actually weep out loud.

What *emotions* did they describe and awaken in you? What was it about the story that appealed to you? What do you remember most? It was probably an emotional moment.

Here are a couple of examples from my own experience.

Pawn in Frankincense by Dorothy Dunnett
There is a scene in this book where the hero Francis Crawford and his opponent have to play a game of chess using real people, including two little boys – Crawford's friends and allies, people he loves – as the pieces. If one of the 'pieces' is captured it means instant death for them. The tension is almost

unbearable, the fear and uncertainty of the characters as they wait for their turn to move jumps off the page. And the horror when they realise that one of the children is in terrible danger is still something that I can hardly bear to read.

Wuthering Heights by Emily Brontë
I still remember feeling Heathcliff's outrage at the way he'd been treated – the burning anger and resentment that, even as a young boy, made sure that he could never, ever forgive. And the terrible unhappiness that came from his own actions, destroying what he most loved.

Gold Ring of Betrayal by Michelle Reid (Mills & Boon Modern Romance 1996)
The moment I always come back to is the hero's struggle to get to know the child – the baby that he doesn't believe is his – the conflict between his pride and his love and his loneliness.

So there you are – lots of emotional words for you:

love	hate	anger
outrage	loneliness	pride
fear	unhappiness	horror

I'd like you to think about some of the books that made you *feel* – that made you understand what I'm talking about here when I'm describing emotional punch. Make notes on them and the memories you have, the way they made you feel when you read them.

Something to write about
▶ Write about yourself.
▶ About your feelings.
▶ About times when you've felt really angry, or sad or happy...
▶ Write down how you felt.
▶ What you thought.
▶ How you saw things – brighter or darker or just differently.
▶ How did you behave?
▶ What did you do to express those emotions?
▶ How did you look? Pale or red in the face? Did you shed tears of joy or refuse to let bitter tears out?
▶ Don't hold back – take the brakes off, no one's going to have to see this – it's private, personal – for you alone. But it will teach you what emotions you feel strongly and deeply and how they affect you. And so how they could affect your characters. And then go on to the next chapter ready to use those feelings when we look at **conflict**.

3

Conflict

I have a problem with 'conflict'. Not with writing it or putting it into books – my characters get very intense about everything and conflict tends to come as naturally to them as breathing. Sometimes the problem I have is in getting them to reconcile at the end and declare their love so that they can have that vital Happy Ever After ending that romances demand. No, the problem I have is with the word itself.

Conflict

Look it up in a dictionary and what do you get?

Conflict – a violent collision – a struggle or contest – a battle – a mental struggle – to fight, contend. To be in opposition. To clash.

When I talk about the conflict in a book, most people are thinking of fights and arguments and battles. And because I write for Modern Romance, they think that 'conflict' means the hero and the heroine arguing, arguing, arguing – throwing insults at each other, never listening to each other, sometimes even physically hurting each other – and then in the last chapter declaring that they love each other, falling into each other's arms and walking off into a sunset... Would you believe that? No, neither would I.

Popular Harlequin Mills & Boon novelists Daphne Clair and Robyn Donald define the conflict as 'the source of tension', and when I'm teaching I prefer to call it 'the problem that is keeping your hero and heroine apart', or 'the thing that stops this couple getting together'. But that ends up being long and complicated – which is why we end up with the shorthand word – conflict.

Why does conflict matter?

Conflict matters – but not conflict as in sniping and arguing and being nasty. Conflict as in there is something that keeps coming between your characters and driving them away from each other when really they want to be together for the rest of their lives. Something that stops them from being totally relaxed with each other, totally committed to each other, totally in love with each other.

Without conflict, you won't have a story. Your hero and heroine will meet, fall in love, marry and live happily ever after. And that will be that. End of story.

There is no emotional tension in such a story. No real emotional punch, because the punch comes from the overcoming of odds against the relationship; the possibility that all may be lost and the story end tragically, not with the happy ever after ending the reader is looking for. Yes, she knows that is what's coming, but she wants to feel that it is possibly at risk, and that this might just be the story that *doesn't* end that way. It is the moments of conflict and their resolution that bring about the emotion that we're trying to get into a book.

Two types of conflict

Conflict can be of two types:

▶ **External conflict**. This is when something or someone outside of the central characters causes the problem that keeps them apart. External conflict is easiest to see in a war situation, say – where your characters are on different sides – Roundheads and Cavaliers in the English Civil War or a German soldier and a French nurse in the Second World War. Or think of Romeo and Juliet when their families were feuding.

An external conflict is outside the hero or heroine, but it still affects them internally, making them grow and change and adapt so that this affects their relationship at the same time.

▶ **Internal conflict**. This arises from the characters' personalities, beliefs, lives, and affects their reactions to the other person. They are usually emotional in origin and are resolved by the characters learning more about each other or themselves and discarding inappropriate beliefs. If we're talking about Shakespeare again – this would be *Othello*, where the conflict or 'the problem' is in Othello's mind; in the fact that deep down he feels unworthy to have the love of Desdemona his wife and so is easily convinced that she is capable of being unfaithful to him.

Internal conflicts are usually made up of some of the emotions we have already looked at – guilt, failure, pride, fear of rejection, the fear that history will repeat itself. These all affect your characters' way of thinking – but quite often they are not even aware of this, which is why these conflicts can complicate matters so much and take so long to unravel.

The best romances are those that have something of both types of conflict in them. An internal conflict is usually a hidden and secret one, so the introduction of an external conflict can bring that out into the open. In the middle of a discussion about something else entirely, people can often reveal what is *really* troubling them – or at least hint at it.

External conflicts can be solved by other, equally external means. A war can come to an end, an arguing family may be reconciled, a liar exposed. But the protagonists' internal dilemmas can only be resolved by the person struggling with them. They have to fight with their own internal demons and overcome them.

A conflict worth fighting over

Conflict has to be worthwhile – it has to be something that would really matter, something worth arguing over, something worth taking the risk of losing the love of your life for. Instant dislike dragged out over almost 200 pages or more soon seems like nothing more than a bad-tempered sulk and will quickly lose your reader's sympathy and interest. Petty arguments, bad temper, temper tantrums, and scene after scene of unreasonable arguments will simply turn your heroine into a whiner or a nasty minded bitch, and your hero into a totally unlovable bully.

Remember, we are writing about modern women who are unlikely to break their hearts over a problem that could quickly be tackled and worked out if she just asked the man involved a couple of questions.

Here, historical writers can have an advantage – things that mattered more in the past can bring in great conflict that a writer of Modern Romance just can't get away with.

So your conflict needs to be something believable, one that matters. Something that your hero and heroine really care about enough to keep fighting over it, keep hurting over it. Something that really means the ruin of their love if they can't resolve it.

Conflict that comes from your characters

The best way to set up a conflict that works is by becoming deeply involved with your hero and heroine, getting to know them as well as you possibly can, and letting the plot come from them, rather than trying to think of a traditional Mills & Boon plot. Lose yourself in their story, write from the heart, and give the novel an emotional edge by making it clear that your hero and heroine have a great deal to lose if their relationship fails. All this will add to the emotional punch of your writing. The deeper the conflict, the more emotional commitment the characters will make to it.

And if the worsening of the conflict, the reversal just at the stage when it looks as if things are going to turn out all right, comes directly from the inadvertent actions of one of the protagonists, then, human nature being what it is, they are likely to be blind to what they've done, or try to cover their tracks, or defend themselves by throwing the blame back onto the other person, and so complicate matters even further.

If your characters have opposing goals, then naturally a conflict will develop from them each trying to achieve the goal that is so important to them. When ideals, aims or beliefs clash, then any one person's progress towards their personal goal must inevitably clash with the other's matching desire. Ultimately this will result in them having to choose between the importance of achieving that goal or having the relationship with the one they love.

Adding layers to a conflict

Very few reasons for conflict, however powerful, can actually last through the whole of a book without changing, adapting, developing, or just varying in tone and emphasis. The best sorts of conflicts are those that have layers and layers of involvement, and as each one is dealt with and peeled away, it reveals another complication, another aspect of the same problem, or a different development of it, going deeper and deeper until finally the central core of the problem is exposed, ready for your characters to tackle it.

This pacing and staging of the revelations that make up the conflict adds to the suspense and the tension that keeps the reader turning the page. It also has the bonus of increasing and building on the sexual tension between the hero and heroine as they want more and more to be together but feel more and more that it will be a mistake/a danger/a disaster.

Long-term and short-term conflicts

Not every conflict needs to be a major one and not every problem is one that lasts through the book. You can vary the pace and the intensity of your story by using long-term and short-term problems. Short-term problems are usually what catapult the hero and heroine together, putting them in a situation in which they have to work out their emotional (long-term) problems.

So if the protagonists were married and have a child, then that child's illness or unhappiness in some way could bring them together and this will then mean that they have to work through the reasons why they separated in the first place. In a thriller for example, the mystery can often be solved well before the emotional relationship has been resolved. These short and long-term problems work well when they are connected and so the difficulties are intertwined.

The long-term problems are usually internal – the result of some character flaw or the scars from past experience – and this is why the character finds some particular short-term problem so very difficult to deal with.

Foreshadowing the conflicts

Basically this means dropping hints or reminders about points of conflict that the reader knows about but perhaps the characters have forgotten or haven't yet discovered. Then, even at a point of what seems like real reconciliation, the reader is aware of the fact that 'She hasn't told him. . .' or 'But he doesn't know that. . .' and this will put an edge of tension onto the scene, knowing that at some point the problem must intrude, or a secret resurface, and wondering just when it will happen and what will result when it does.

And if you can drop in a comment or a thought that reflects the probable reaction that will follow, then this turns the tension up another notch and increases the nervous anticipation at the same time.

Contrived plots and undeveloped conflicts

A contrived plot is often one that has been overused or one that might have had its day but now has lost much of its impact because society has changed so that it no longer seems quite so believable any more.

An example of this is the overworked 'other woman' plot. This can be more difficult to bring in and make it work because people are much more open with each other and because young women are now much more up-front and forthright. Today's heroines are no longer naïve innocents or wimps.

So it would be difficult to believe that any modern young woman would seriously believe her husband/fiancé/lover was being unfaithful to her just because she saw him once with another woman in a restaurant or in the street. And this is a plot twist that soon runs out of steam – why doesn't she just confront him and demand an explanation?

Of course, if the problem is compounded by her own lack of self-esteem, and when she raises her fears, they then open up other problems and differences of goals then it can be developed from this point. An undeveloped conflict is one where there aren't enough genuine differences and problems between the characters to maintain the distance between them and to keep the reader interested.

Building up to a crisis

The tension and the conflict in your story should also grow, escalate, building upwards more and more strongly. You need to build up the heat, emotionally, sexually and dramatically between your central characters. If you give your hero and heroine problems then those problems should get progressively worse, either through outside influences as yet another reason for them to be on opposite sides is discovered, or a family member intervenes, or outside forces turn the tide against them. Or their own actions make things worse so that they move further and further apart.

Don't forget that any moment of tension, any argument or split that drives your protagonists apart will feel all the worse if it comes just after, or intrudes into some moment when it looked as if they were actually reaching some understanding, a reconciliation, or at least giving each other a chance to explain. If something then happens to distract them from this reconciliation, their chances of resolution – or at least some improvement in circumstances – is destroyed and they are as far apart as ever.

This means that the 'line' of the novel should move in zigzags, like the letter W –

going up through tension to a painful pitch, then coming down to a more peaceful stage, only to shoot upwards again as something new is added – two steps forward, one step back.

The whole movement of the conflict builds and builds towards the major final conflict in which it looks as if nothing will ever be the same again and the hero and heroine will never ever be able to resolve their differences. It seems that all is lost for ever.

This point is usually known as the 'Black Moment' and we will look at this moment in Chapter 12.

12 questions about conflict

1. Have I created a conflict that is truly worth being at odds over? One that really matters?

2. Do I understand my characters well enough so that this conflict comes from within them, is entirely personal to them and so is believable in their responses to it?

3. Does my conflict have 'layers' like an onion so that, if you peel away or deal with one part of it, there are still other old or new conflicts revealed needing to be dealt with?

4. Do the conflicts flow naturally together and tangle up to create a stronger, more difficult problem?

5. Is the conflict appropriate to the period and the setting in which my book takes place?

6. Do I have both internal and external conflicts?

7. Do my characters have both long-term and short-term problems that are related to each other?

8. Do the problems build believably and progressively until they create the 'Black Moment' when everything seems to be lost?

9. Is the resolution of the conflict a natural outcome of the events of the plot and the characters' personalities? No *deus ex machina* or magician waving a magic wand to solve everything. How do the main characters contribute to the solution of their own problems?

10. Have I resolved all the conflicts and subplots by the end of the book?

11. No matter what other conflicts, problems or mysteries have to be dealt with, is the development of the romance in the story paramount in the novel and the emotional climax the one that matters?

12. If other people have been involved in the conflict – parents, family, villains or 'other woman' – have I dealt with them satisfactorily or just 'shuffled them off, stage left'?

Exercises

Something to think about

You have already thought about books you know from the **emotion** point of view – now I'd like you to think about stories you've read where the **conflict** hit you hard and affected you strongly.

I want you to think about conflict that you – as the person you are, the age you are, living in the place you do, in the century you're in – would find believable. And ones that just don't work for you. I also want you to look at the different sorts of conflict – the degrees of conflict. For example:

In Michelle Reid's *The Sheikh's Chosen Wife* (M&B Modern 2002) – initially the conflict is external – the society in which the Sheikh lives demands that his wife gives him a son – his wife cannot give him a child – so even though they love each other desperately, this is tearing them apart. But there's more to it than that – the way their love for each other is a source of conflict too – because of it Leona wants to do what is best for Hassan – by leaving – and because of it Hassan is determined not to let her go.

Or try Anne McAllister's *The Inconvenient Bride* (M&B Modern 2001). Dominic and Sierra aren't at loggerheads. They don't hate each other. They fancy the pants off each other. And they get married. But it's the *why* they get married that brings the problem and is the source of conflict. If you want an example of how conflict doesn't have to be angry, aggressive or hostile but can undermine the strength of a relationship all the same – try this one.

Or try my own book, *His Miracle Baby* (M&B Modern 2001) – where again two people were madly in love – but Morgan's determination never to have children tore them apart. And when they meet up again, first the secret baby, and then the fact that Ellie now has his child keeps coming between them. When Ellie discovers *why* Morgan made that decision in the first place it only adds to the conflict.

For historical stories try Joanna Maitland's *Marrying the Major* (M&B Historical 2002). It has a plot that turns on the fact that the heroine is seen kissing another man. In 2004 that would be a very minor conflict – depending on the type of kiss! – but during the Regency it meant that a woman was ruined; her reputation was destroyed for ever – a very different situation.

Any books where you just didn't believe the conflict are also worth also looking at. If you can work out why they don't work for you then you will know what scenarios to avoid in your own writing. And if you can come up with changes that would make you believe in them then you're learning a lot about plotting by doing so.

Something to write about

Your writing as a result of the previous chapter has shown you some of the things that make you feel emotions. But which ones would you fight to the bitter end for – and risk everything?

Start thinking of this as the basis for a plot – we're going to be looking at characters soon – the hero and heroine – so to put them into a plot you're going to need a point of conflict. I don't normally work this way – usually I get my hero and heroine's characters first and then see what would split them apart – but as we're looking at how much a conflict matters, I'm approaching it this way for once. So in your writing, think of a reason for being at odds. Something that would create a conflict.

Write down several ideas – and ask yourself why would this matter – why would he or she believe it? Why would they fight over it? For example – I often critique manuscripts where the heroine believes that the hero has been unfaithful to her. Now, as I've already discussed, this is a tricky one – if she just believes someone else's lies and never challenges him, she can appear naïve and silly. If she finds him in bed with someone else – then that's pretty good proof – but this is the *hero* – so if he's going to be found in bed with someone else, you need to have a very strong reason for that happening. And you need a good reason why they don't just argue about it and clear the air right then and there.

Conflict doesn't just happen – it has reasons and complications and it develops and changes. So ask yourself those questions and write down the answers. If you want to take it further, and you're feeling like going for it – you can put that conflict into dialogue between the two characters.

In the next chapter we'll deal with dialogue in detail.

4

Dialogue

When I first started out as a published writer, my editor gave me the 'rule of thumb' that a pacy, page-turning novel should be 60% dialogue and 40% narrative. I see that the editors are still stating the same proportions – so it seems a good place to start.

Why is dialogue so important?

Well, you know that old saying about writing – 'show don't tell'? I'm always being asked what that means and how to do it. And one of the simplest answers to the question is – **dialogue**.

Dialogue is the lifeblood of your novel. It brings characters to life and makes them spring off the page and into your reader's imagination. It shows mood, brings pace, adds variety. It gives information in a palatable form and shows how the person revealing that information feels about it. It adds drama, makes the reading experience vivid, moving the story along. And it stops your reader from becoming aware that they are reading a book.

Does that sound like a contradiction? Not really. If your reader becomes aware that they are reading – in other words, if something jolts them out of the story – a word they just can't understand – the use of the wrong name for a hero or heroine (it does happen), a factual mistake – they are likely to pause, think 'Oh I really should be doing something else' – or 'it's time for sleep' or something similar. They'll put the book down – and maybe never pick it up again. A book that can easily be put down is often not a memorable one.

Adding drama through dialogue

Dialogue drags the reader into the book because it makes them feel that they are present at the scene they're reading about. They 'hear' the voices of your characters – or they should do if you write them well – and it's like being at a play, watching the action unfold in front of them.

Narrative doesn't do this. Narrative immediately slows things down, it makes the reader aware of great chunks of solid text on the page – and all too often narrative gets skipped over and on to the good bits – the dramatic bits – and the dramatic bits are made dramatic by the dialogue.

It can also deceive the reader and other characters. Just think of how interesting it can be to have your character saying one thing and then thinking something totally different. The person they are speaking to is totally unaware of these thoughts and so in blissful ignorance about the truth. The reader, however, is well aware of them and so has an extra thrill that comes from an added tension – a form of conflict that the character doesn't know about.

Make it fit your characters
The important thing about dialogue is that it needs to be *in character*.

▶ It's no good saying that Mr Jones has a biting, sarcastic wit if he never uses it. Or saying that Miss Jones is a very stupid, slow-witted girl if she continually uses multi-syllabled words and complicated sentences. People also have pet phrases, expressions they use, they might swear heavily – or be prim and proper, old-fashioned or very very trendy – or speaking a particular form of slang. You need to reflect this in the way they speak. So the basic rule is:
  – know what your characters do and why they do it
  – know what your characters say and how they say it.

There are a couple of other important things to remember about dialogue.

▶ It needs to sound **realistic**. People talking – especially people talking in some emotional situation – don't speak in perfectly grammatical, coherent sentences. They stop and start, break off, change verbal direction, repeat themselves. And they don't use the full form of words unless it's for a particular reason. They'd say 'don't' rather than 'do not' or 'I can't' rather than 'I cannot'. It might seem obvious but it isn't always so. If you're not sure if your dialogue reads realistically, try reading it aloud. If you stumble over the sentences or end up laughing or find that you have to read it in an artificial way then it's not working.

▶ In a novel the dialogue **needs to say something**. That sounds obvious but if you'd seen the number of times I've read:

'Hello Jane.'
'Oh hello, Tom. Nice morning, isn't it?'
'Yes but I think it might rain later...'

And the conversation continues on this level for pages, then you'd see what I mean. Dialogue in a book, especially in short novel like a romance, can't be wasted. It needs to *do* something.

▶ **Your characters need to do something as well**. If you have long, long conversations that are just dialogue, going back and forth between your characters, then two things can happen. Firstly, the reader can get lost;

she's not sure who's speaking right at this moment. And secondly, all the physical reality of your characters can evaporate as the reader loses track of where they are and what they're doing. So you need to put in what the acting world calls 'business'. You need to visualise the scene as it's happening and think about the actions your characters will make, the hand gestures, the things they'll pick up, put down, the way they'll move about the room. So not just:

'Good morning.'
'Nice day isn't it?'
'Yes, but I think it will rain later.'

But:

'Good morning,' Jonathan said, coming into the kitchen and letting the door swing to behind him.
Mary glanced up from where she was washing plates in the sink.
'Nice day isn't it?'
'Yes.' Jonathan nodded, his dark eyes taking in the mess on the table. 'But I think it will rain later.'

He said; she said

Everyone seems to get hung up on whether to put in 'tags' – i.e. whether to add 'he said' or 'she said' and even more hung up on whether to add anything else, such as:

'She murmured seductively.'
'He shouted furiously.'

There's only one rule: **Don't bore or frustrate your reader!**

► If you keep on saying he said/she said after every piece of dialogue, you'll bore your reader.

► If you keep on describing *how* it was said – angrily or quietly – it will bore your reader.

► But also if they can't work out if it was Jonathan or Mary who spoke then that will frustrate them, particularly if they have to read back, counting the lines of dialogue and saying 'Mary' 'Jonathan' to see who said what it will frustrate them intensely.

▶ And if they can't quite be sure just *how* something was meant that will frustrate them too.

If you write dialogue properly, it should be obvious *how* something is said – 'I hate you!' shouldn't need to have ' she said angrily' tagged on to the end of it.

But if she said 'I hate you' in a very different way – quietly, despairingly, meaning in fact the opposite then you need to add some words to describe just that.

Remember that variety is the spice of dialogue, just as it is in life. Put in some 'saids', and other words like 'growled', 'shrieked', 'flung at him' as appropriate – but not on every line. Scatter them about. Use them where you feel they will add information, explanation or just more interest. Just like conversation in real life!

12 questions about dialogue

1. Do I have approximately 60% dialogue to 40% narrative?

2. Does the dialogue I use fit the characters I have given it to?

3. Does the dialogue serve a purpose – does it further the plot or add to the reader's knowledge about the characters or explain something that has happened in the past or the back story?

4. Do my characters have bits of 'business' or movement to do in amongst the dialogue so that they are not just talking heads but real people centred in a place the reader can see in their mind?

5. Does the dialogue pass the 'read aloud' test? Does it sound natural and realistic?

6. Have I used language appropriate to the period and place that the book is set?

7. If I have a non-English hero or heroine have I used their dialogue to indicate this by phrasing, arrangement of words or accurate use of their native language?

8. Does the dialogue show the mood of the character by the way they speak?

9. Does the dialogue differ slightly for each person so that the reader can guess who is speaking?

10. Is the dialogue apposite to the speaker's age, status and relationship to the person they are speaking to?

11. Have I overloaded the text with 'he saids' or other words such as 'shouted', 'declared', 'expostulated', etc?

12. Can I cut out any unnecessary adverbs and leave the dialogue to stand on its own and still have the emotion show clearly?

Exercises

Something to think about

For this exercise, you have to become a spy – or as I usually call it – the writer as magpie.

You are going to snoop into people's conversations whether in your home, on the train into work, in the shops, even on the TV. You're going to listen in, see how they speak, watch the gestures they make, the words they repeat over and over.

And you're going to try to find words to describe what they're doing. See if you can guess what mood they're in. What their relationship is with the person they're talking to.

In other words, you're going to watch dialogue happening and make notes, mental or physical, about it so that you can use them in your writing.

Something to write about

Remember the conflict you came up with for the last chapter? Now I want you to write a few lines of dialogue about it – several times – but each time it has to be slightly different.

1. Just stating the basic conflict.

2. Putting in some emotion – how is it said? Make the words sound right, with the right mood behind them. How does each person react?

3. Putting in some 'business' so that the people talking can also be 'seen' by the reader.

And then – do it again, but this time with two totally different characters.

If your first dialogue is between, say, a boss and his secretary (you can make whichever one you like male or female) then the second exercise has perhaps a father and a daughter, or a shop assistant and a customer, or a teacher and the father of one of his or her pupils.

Choose any characters you like. Just make them different from the first pair of characters and see how differently their dialogue will come out when they discuss the same topic.

5

Focus

The full wording of this point should read 'Sharp focus on the hero and heroine'.

Focus means intensity

This is one area where romance can differ from other genres. And the reason for this is obvious – it's because of the motivation that pushes a reader to pick up a romance. She does so because she wants to read the story of how two people meet, their emotional journey, the conflict that keeps them apart, until they reach that happy ever after ending.

So if the reader wants to see that relationship then she will want the spotlight to be on it as much of the time as possible.

Clearly, if you are writing a thriller, a romantic suspense novel or a historical romance, then there will have to be time spent on other events, other characters and other details. And if you are involved in creating a much longer book – a 'saga' for example, where there are perhaps several generations of the same family, then this is not a hard and fast rule. But in romance, and particularly the 'category romances' it's much more important.

I write for Harlequin Mills and Boon Modern Romance (Harlequin Presents in America) and that means that I have to keep up a strong, emotional intensity throughout the book. There are those who believe that Presents heroes and heroines have to be fighting and arguing all the time and that's where the 'intensity' comes from. This is not so. The intensity comes from concentrating the spotlight on the heroine and the hero together, and the way that they interact, not diffusing it and diluting the impact by bringing in other things. So what can dilute that focus?

Other characters

In bigger books, a huge cast of characters can help to 'people' the story. They can bring their own stories along, mirror the main stories you're telling, add complications, give more historical detail. But in a category romance you only have 55,000 words in which to tell the whole story, to let the characters get to know each other, to develop and resolve that conflict. If you bring in other characters, all with their own stories to tell, their own personalities to display, then your heroine or your hero can get lost in the crowd.

Of course there are some lines where this is not quite so important. In America, Superromance, for example, can bring in a larger 'cast'. And series like Harlequin Intrigue need to have villains and suspects to further the thriller plots. Even in a shorter romance, you might need a few 'supporting characters' – the heroine's boyfriend or mother, the hero's brother, their child if it's a 'Secret Baby' plot – but they should be sketched in lightly and not take centre stage. Secondary characters, and scenes between them and hero or heroine, and not with each other dilute the tension, slow the pace and dilute the focus.

Flashbacks
With some stories, a flashback is vital. If the main characters have met before, and the past events have shaped who they are and how they feel about each other, then clearly it's vital to bring it in. But if you are not careful, flashbacks can take over from the present day telling of the story. The reader can get so tangled in it that they lose their focus on what is actually happening in the present.

It's in the present that the problems are being worked out and solved. You should consider carefully whether you really need the detail in the flashback that you want to include. Often a reader thinks, 'Well, I know what happened – I can work it out from what they're saying to each other. I don't need to *see* it.'

If going 'back' is vital, it can often be done perfectly when the hero and heroine talk about the past. That way it's still vivid, alive and in the present. The central characters stay together, the conversation is shown and the way that each person reacts and changes their opinions as the story is told is an important part of character growth.

If you still need to recount some of the story in the past, then stick to the events that actually affected the conflict and don't spend time embroidering them with unnecessary details. Get back to the present as soon as possible. And try not to put huge solid chunks of back story but thread the details *through* the story.

Narrative
We've already looked at this under dialogue (Chapter 4). Narrative slows a book down. It tells, it doesn't show. Dialogue gives it pace, life, immediacy. It shows the scene, making it come alive, and it focuses the attention on the speaker, just as talking to them in real life would. And it brings across the character of the protagonists so vividly.

Some narrative is inevitable, but, again, avoid large chunks of it that reduce the intensity of the focus you are looking for.

Separation
I have read some so-called romances in which the hero and heroine meet, the story starts, and then the hero disappears for pages and pages. Again, this means that the book loses much of its impact and the longer they stay away the worse it gets.

This is one of the problems of the romance genre – keeping your main characters together, even if they hate the sight of each other. Why do you think marriages of convenience stories are so popular – they just can't get away.

If you watch soap operas on TV, you will notice that one of the most frequently repeated scenes is where one character walks out on another – usually leaving the character left behind just calling the other's name in a vain attempt to bring them back. But then when they do meet up again, they are simply shown together and it goes on from there. In a book, you are going to have to find a reason why these two would actually be back in the same room, the same house, the same town, even the same country, given the jet-setting lifestyle of many of today's romance heroes.

So if you need to put a separation in between your hero and heroine, make sure it's as brief as possible (at least in pages – you can make it months in fact, but don't force the reader to sit through every one of those days!) And then have a reason for them getting back together.

This is why the isolation storylines can work well – like being trapped in a snowed-in cottage (I've used that at least twice in *Game of Hazard* and *Fiancée By Mistake*). The hero and heroine can't move away from each other so they *have* to talk.

Whose point of view do you use?

The use of point of view (pov) is another way of providing an even more intense focus on the character you want to reveal to the reader. You not only show them speaking and in action but you reveal their thoughts, filtering the action through them.

The point of view is the vantage point from which the action and events is observed. In fiction, it refers to the angle from which the story is told. The viewpoint character is the one whose perspective on the scene is given. We read the events filtered through the thoughts and opinions of that person.

Three different viewpoints
The different points of view are defined in this way:

▶ **First person.** This is when story is told by a character in his or her own words. The character will use the words 'I', 'we', etc. Using this viewpoint brings immediacy and personal impact to the writing but you must be careful only ever to let the person report things that they can see or have personal knowledge of. As a result, large parts of the action may be hidden from them.

▶ **Second person**. The author uses the pronouns 'you' and 'yours', making the reader into the main character. This can have a personal appeal and directness but it can sound lecturing and needs skilful handling.

▶ **Third person**. An anonymous narrator observes the characters and reports the action using their names and 'his', 'her', etc. The narrator observes all the action of the story and can move into the thoughts and feelings of one or more of the characters.

This viewpoint is most often used for a romance, with the thoughts and feelings of either just the heroine or both the heroine and the hero shown to the reader.

Changes in use of viewpoint in romance

It used to be the convention that only the heroine's point of view was ever shown to the reader. The hero usually kept his thoughts to himself and as a result remained mysterious and distant until the last chapter or so when he declared his love for the heroine.

This meant that the author had to use other ways to show the reader that the hero was moving from a position of hostility, aggression or even hatred, to falling in love. As a result, his actions would only be seen through the heroine's eyes and the reader would share in her mistakes and misapprehensions, judging him as cruel and mean, when perhaps he wasn't.

Long-term readers of romance would be used to reading the clues scattered through the story and so be able to interpret the hero's actions in a different light from that of the heroine. But this technique could result in the hero appearing cruel and unapproachable, and so unlovable, and as a result the reputation of the Alpha Mills and Boon hero as a brute and thug grew up.

It was thought that to show the hero's point of view would reduce his mystery to the reader, give away vital points of the plot and so reduce the appeal of the romance. But in fact the opposite has proved to be the case. Readers love to be let inside the minds of the heroes in these stories, to see what motivates them and why they are behaving as they are. So the modern romance writer needs to choose which point of view to use, whether to use more than one, and when to change it.

How to choose which viewpoint to use

When you are considering whether to use the hero or the heroine's point of view, these are some of the points you should think about to help you decide.

▶ Who tells the story?

▶ Whose story is this?

▶ What kind of information must be shared?

▶ With whom do we want the reader to sympathise?

▶ What information is it most important to give the reader in this scene?

▶ Who possesses that information?

▶ Will the impact of that information be greater if they get it directly from the character who holds that secret, or if they're taken off guard when the non-pov character shares his knowledge?

▶ Which character has the most at stake in this scene?

▶ Whose thoughts and reactions are the most important?

▶ How can you best preserve any surprise or mystery that occurs in the scene or book?

It has been said that it is best to look at a scene, or a point in a scene, from the point of view of the character who has the most to lose at that moment. I would also add to this that it can be most effective to use the following.

▶ The character who is feeling the strongest at this particular moment.

▶ The one whose thoughts are in opposition to what they are saying.

▶ When one character knows more about the situation than the other, then you will need to weigh up whether it is more effective to let your reader know that information – in which case you will be in the head of the person with that knowledge – or hide it from them by being in the head of the person hearing the information, and so taking it on face value.

In this way, using viewpoint and moving from one to another is a highly effective tool to increase reader sympathy and connection with the characters.

Head-hopping

Some authors believe that it is wrong to 'head-hop' – i.e. change point of view frequently from one character to another within the same scene, and on several occasions. There are those who say that a writer should only ever show one character's point of view in each scene, and should change point of view only at the change of scenes, but I don't think that is a terrible sin in writing romance. Not these days.

There are some conventions that have their day and then the genre moves on and leaves them behind – and if you're not careful it can also leave you (as a writer) way behind. It's similar to the way that readers who haven't looked at a romance since about 1960 will say that the heroines are all virgins and the story always stops well outside the bedroom door – and we all know how dated that idea is! The use of point of view is one of these.

Many, if not most, novels are now written from the dual viewpoint of the hero and the heroine, some from the hero's point of view only. My opinion is that this makes for much more interesting reading and writing.

As an example, I wrote a book called *A Sicilian Husband* (Mills & Boon Modern Romance 2003). This book wouldn't have worked without the hero's viewpoint. He was behaving in one way and thinking in another, entirely different way. The only way to show the contrast between what he was saying and what he was thinking and planning was by writing it. I loved writing it and a lot of people wrote to me to tell me how much they enjoyed reading it.

Along with the death of the 'heroine's viewpoint only' convention, then the one point of view to one scene goes out the window too. In my opinion, you can change viewpoint as much as you need in a scene, a chapter, a book – but you need to follow a few pointers:

▶ As stated above, it's usually best to write from the point of view of the person whose thoughts are most important for the reader to know. This is often described as the person with the most to lose – in other words – the person who is feeling the most intensely at the moment you're writing about.

▶ The reader doesn't want to feel as if she's at an emotional tennis match. You don't want her to feel that she switching from A to B to A to B with each speech and each line until she becomes dizzy and confused, so pace it. Just as we discussed in Chapter 4, when talking about dialogue, you need to ground the changes so that your reader knows what's going on. And just as with dialogue, you can use actions and 'business' to help with this.

▶ Make sure that you make it clear just *whose* viewpoint you're using. So if you change the viewpoint put in a line such as '...Rafael thought grimly' or '...Louise told herself...' so that it's plain who is thinking what.

▶ In a short romance it's usually better just to have the central characters' point of view – the hero's and the heroine's and no one else's. You can introduce other ones but in a short book this can dilute the impact of your main protagonists and this is where the tension comes from.

▶ Try to balance out the viewpoint sections evenly. Don't have all the hero's point of view for pages and pages and then just one line of the heroine's feelings before dashing back to the hero – give them equal shares! Introduce the two viewpoints early on in the book and then give them a balanced exposure after that.

▶ Remember that you are showing the thoughts and feelings of two separate people, so write their viewpoints in character as well. Your hero's thoughts should be very different in tone and attitude from those of your heroine.

If you remember these points, then I think you'll see that most romance novels 'hop' from one viewpoint to another as best suits their story. After all, that's what it's about – using the techniques available to create the best possible and most intensely dramatic story.

12 questions about focus

1. Have I studied the use of focus in other books in this line to learn as much as I can about it?

2. Are my hero and heroine at the forefront of the story for the majority of the book?

3. Have I kept my hero and heroine together as much as possible and only separated them when it is vital to the story?

4. If it is not possible for them to be together, have I kept the missing person in the reader's mind as much as possible?

5. Have I kept secondary characters to a minimum, except in books that welcome them and where I have them have I used them to mirror or forward the central emotional plot of the hero and heroine?

6. Have I put in flashbacks only when really necessary and kept them as vivid as possible?

7. Have I avoided long passages of narrative and description?

8. Have I used the viewpoint of the character whose feelings are most important?

9. Have I made it clear when I am changing viewpoint and from whose point of view I am switching?

10. Have I made use of the viewpoint to add to the reader's knowledge of the character whose thoughts are shown, but making sure I haven't included anything this character couldn't have known?

11. Have I written the viewpoint of the hero differently from the heroine's point of view?

12. Have I used viewpoint to show the characters' emotional development, their changing feelings and their mistaken beliefs?

Exercises

Something to think about

We've looked at the way that places and other people and separations can diffuse the tension that you need to have in a romance novel, so here are some things I'd like you to think about.

Try to imagine some places where you could set your story – and the difficulties involved in focusing on your heroine and hero there.

We've already mentioned the isolated, snowed-in cottage but there are plenty of others:

▶ The boss and secretary have to spend long hours in the same office, or at least next door.

▶ A tiny island.

▶ Or what about the Sheikh books? They are not just so popular because of the type of hero (and we're coming to that later) but because the heroine will be isolated and out of her depth in the desert environment. And that feeling of being out of her depth will make her more vulnerable to the hero.

▶ And that can be reversed – with, say, a sophisticated Italian businessman hero trapped on a Yorkshire farm where the weather, the conditions, the language/dialect all make him feel out of his depth.

Lynne Graham's novel *Prisoner of Passion* (Mills & Boon Modern 1996) in which the hero and heroine are trapped in a huge metal cell for a couple of chapters. There is no escape, no privacy – and they are forced to get to know each other pretty quickly!

Try to think of situations in which you can 'trap' your characters. This setting of a story can add an extra dimension of conflict and tension just by where they are. So it's worth thinking about it and not just setting your book 'in a big city.'

Also think about that moment when 'he stormed out, slamming the door behind him'. What reasons can you think of to get them back together and so keep the focus fully on them?

To study the use of point of view, take another look at the books you've read. See whose viewpoint is used and where in each scene.

Why do you think it's the heroine (or the hero) whose point of view is given in each scene?

How would it change your view of the scene if the other person's viewpoint was used?

Something to write about

We've worked on conflict, emotion, dialogue and focus, together with point of view – so why not try putting all of this together? Think of a conversation where your hero and heroine are talking about the reasons for their conflict – and add a setting. Now write that conversation, taking into account the setting where it's taking place. How does this affect your hero and your heroine? How would it change if it was set somewhere else? Try it. What would happen if you were to introduce another character or a lot of other characters? See if you can find ways of keeping these other characters as just shadows so that they don't intrude. What would happen if one or more did intrude? Sometimes it can add to the tension as well as dilute it.

Finally, try to write this from both points of view – your heroine's and your hero's. See what differences this will make and how each of them feels and thinks about things.

6

Sensuality

Sensuality doesn't just mean putting the steam in – and writing the love scenes, the sexy bits. That's part of it. But it's not all of it, not by a long way.

Obviously, passion, which is the next chapter's topic, and sensuality are very closely linked. But if you have one without the other you end up with a very strange, unbalanced story. If you have passion without sensuality to lead up to it, then it will seem cold, awkward, and out of place, as if it's just been put there to titillate and not as a serious, important part of the romance.

Because that's what a love scene in a romance should be. We're not writing erotica here – nor, by any stretch of the imagination, is romance pornography. It's a romance and because of that, as we've already discussed, the emotion must be uppermost in it. Which is why we started with emotion, and sensuality has only just made its appearance.

Sensuality appropriate for the line

Sensuality may seem to be a topic that would only be discussed in relation to a Modern/Presents novel – or a Blaze, say. In the more modern and sophisticated lines. Don't you believe it! There may be many different degrees of sensuality in romances – from a Betty Neels hero who might just pat his heroine's hand and kiss her hard – to the hot-blooded sexual power of a Miranda Lee or the Blaze authors.

The first thing you need to find out is the appropriate level of sensuality for the line you particularly want to write for – the line you plan on targeting. Once again, the only way you'll ever learn that is by *reading*. Read, read, and read. Read as many different authors as you can find. And judge for yourself what works in each line – and the varying degrees of sensuality within even one of those lines.

There are no rules or 'writing by numbers'

Too many people believe there are rules and regulations for what can happen in a romance. I've even had someone tell me that there is a strict 'rule book' where it states which parts of the body can be touched and how and when – clothed or unclothed – and what sort of kiss.

Can you imagine how it would feel to write like that? Like those painting by numbers kits that used to be on sale. 'If this is the second kiss then maybe they can open their mouths...'

The way to find out the truth is – once again – to read.

So once you've read a variety of authors in your chosen line, you'll get an idea of what's wanted. The next thing is to make sure that *you* are comfortable with what you're trying to write. If you get the giggles at seeing the word 'nipple' or 'buttocks' in print, then you're not going to be able to launch into a Presents or a Blaze without awkwardness. Don't force yourself to write what you can't do – but accept that there are some lines you might just not be happy to write in.

Building a sensual picture

Sensuality starts out as just interest – and builds from there. This is why you'll find that most romances are full of colours, textures, descriptions of all sorts.

The hero's eyes might be emerald green/gleaming bronze/deepest brown/ sapphire blue. The heroine's hair could be a golden blonde/burnished copper/ fiery red/jet black... There are descriptions of physique, of legs, of hands, of hair... All these serve two purposes.

1. To put the hero and heroine firmly in front of the reader's 'mental eye' – to have them envisioning the characters fully in their imagination.

2. To build up, maintain and then develop the sensual awareness of each other – an awareness that grows and builds and gets bigger and bigger until it's a raging fire that can't be controlled.

The first four minutes
When writing descriptions, remember that psychologists say that we tend to judge, assess and form our opinions of someone in the first four minutes after we meet them. So when you are creating images of your main characters try to keep this in mind. You could test it out the next time you meet someone for the first time. Note what you really noticed about them, and make your heroine register the sort of things that hit home in those first four minutes.

Creating characters who are not 'perfect'

People complain that romance heroes and heroines are always perfect, always 'tall, dark and handsome' or 'slim, curvaceous, beautiful'. But what they forget is that the hero is seen through the heroine's eyes and vice versa. These characters are supposed to be each other's once-in-a-lifetime love – so it would be crazy if they didn't find each other devastatingly attractive.

There are plenty of books where the physical descriptions are not just the stereotypes – but too many people go by the covers on the books, and the model types shown there.

I have had heroes who have had scarred faces (*Fiancée By Mistake* M&B Modern 1998), or have been injured so that they're left with a bad limp (*Man of Shadows* M&B 1987). Incidentally, Jordan, the hero in *Man of Shadows* is also described as not being as tall as a couple of other men who appear in the story and having 'a compact strength'. But you wouldn't know that from the cover. In the same way, heroes or heroines who wear spectacles rarely have them on in the cover picture.

Very often a hero is described as having a strong, rawboned face, which isn't conventionally handsome, but again most people will go by the handsome male models on the covers. When a reader is involved in your story she will create her own mental image of the hero and heroine, but in order to do this she needs details of colouring of hair and eyes, body build and height.

It is possible to have an unconventional or rather unusual type of man or woman as your central character, but remember that if you do you may have to work harder to make sure that they appeal to your reader. The reason 'tall, dark and handsome' has become an overworked cliché in romance is because it is a neat form of shorthand for the sort of man generally accepted as attractive.

But the unconventional works is when it's an important part of the plot of the book as a whole. Anne McAllister created a wonderful non-typical heroine in Sierra in *The Inconvenient Bride*. Sierra had purple hair and she married a very hard-headed businessman – and the plot grew perfectly out of their differences.

Filling in the details

You can describe your hero and heroine how you like – but keep building up the sensual impression. Use colours, clothes, the texture of materials, the way they move, the jewellery, make-up worn (presumably just by the heroine! I haven't yet found any heroes who dress as drag queens!).

Then you add some physical details – scent can be very important. It could be the scent of someone's skin or hair, not just the perfume they wear. Scent is a very evocative way to bring back a memory. The scent of someone left on the sheets of a bed, the way that a leather jacket can smell after it's been in the rain.

Use all the other senses too:

▶ Hearing – the sound of a voice, an accent.

▶ Taste – of skin – of food eaten while sitting opposite the hero or heroine.

▶ Sight – we've already dealt with so many things you can see. I'm sure you can think of more.

▶ Put in actions – the touch of hand on hand – the stroke of fingers over hair or down a cheek – a smile – a glance – even a laugh.

▶ And don't forget the surroundings. The place where your hero and heroine are. Again, colours and textures – or the scent of flowers, newly mown grass in a garden – the tang of the ocean on the wind – the feel of sand under bare feet. The touch of the sheets on bare skin – but are those sheets satin, silk or crisp fresh cotton?

Geographical settings

The setting of your novel is as much about sensuality as the physical details and responses of your hero and heroine. The setting adds to the overall mood and atmosphere of the book and enhances the impact of the characters too.

Once again, you need to read and study the lines to see what sort of setting they want in their stories. Modern Romance (Presents in America) has a reputation for using sophisticated and international settings. They often have Mediterranean heroes – Italian, Spanish, Greek, Sicilian – and the action of the book can take place in international cities.

Please note – I said *can take place*. This doesn't mean that a book will automatically be barred from this line if it is set somewhere quieter and less sophisticated. Strangely enough, I am constantly being asked by UK writers if Modern Romances will allow UK settings – while the American and Canadian authors ask if American and Canadian settings will work.

The truth is that any setting will work. But as with the 'tall, dark and handsome' shorthand, a warm, sunny and exotic place is easier to make sensual and exciting than a small Yorkshire village in a snowstorm.

But I've used both and plenty of other places.

Settings should not be a travel guide
When you are creating an exotic setting for your story, there are some points you should remember:

▶ You are not writing a travelogue, so the background you want to use needs to be sketched in with a light hand – just enough to give a flavour and atmosphere. You'll be amazed how much can be done with a hot sun and the scent of a particular plant for example. Readers like to use their imagination too.

▶ A setting is just that – a place for things to happen. The background, however exotic, should never intrude or take over the plot of the book that is the development of the romance. As Michelle Reid says – 'The setting is just an address where the couple go to talk about things.'

▶ Think about the ways that different settings will affect the action of the plot. A snowbound cottage will have one effect on the characters; a hot, lush Caribbean island can have a very different one.

Settings always come second

I once gave a talk on writing romance and afterwards a lady came up to me and said could she ask a question. She said that she had travelled a lot, been on a lot of cruises, etc, so she knew she could write a brilliant romance. All she had to do was to decide which place to set it – so did I think it would be best to use the cruise in Egypt or the Italian villa, or the Greek island?

But do you have a story? I asked. Characters?

Oh no, she said, but that won't matter will it? It's the exotic setting they want and I can just put any old romance in there.

Unfortunately, she was going about things back to front. You want to think of your characters first, then add in the conflict that makes a plot, then if a Mediterranean setting, or the Bahamas or somewhere else works you can move your characters there.

But a wonderful, exotic setting will never make up for a dull, uninspired plot and cardboard characters. If your hero is flat and one-dimensional in Yorkshire, he'll be flat and one dimensional in Marrakech or Mesopotamia or Sicily or Turkey. It's the characters that matter, then you can put them into a setting.

Even if your characters are in some foreign country – or just in the heroine's backyard – or some small cottage in Cumbria, it's what's happening that matters and the setting can be a plus but it certainly won't make up for any lack in the more important things.

You need to think about what your setting is adding to the story. And then you need to do your research carefully, get your facts right – but remember that light hand.

Sensuality builds up tension

And all this can add to the PTQ. As sensual effect piles on effect and the build up mounts and the tension becomes stronger (tension is something we'll come back to when we look at passion in the next chapter) you will have both your reader and your hero and heroine moving along with you in a state of anticipation and expectancy.

Because much of the time it's anticipation, rather than action that is the exciting part – once the passion has come to a head then there can be a lull afterwards. But we'll come to that in the next chapter.

12 questions about sensuality

1. Have I created vivid physical pictures of my hero and heroine?

2. Have I given the characters individual traits (scars, glasses, big feet) and so stopped them from being just clichés – tall, dark, handsome or slim, blonde, beautiful?

3. Have I built images of the settings, the rooms, the country where the story takes place, using colour and texture and scents?

4. Have I used all five senses?

5. If I were to describe someone in those 'first four minutes' what details would I remember most and what would most affect me?

6. What characters do I connect with particular colourings and how would these affect the way I create and write about my characters?

7. Have I used images to enhance the descriptions I've given – emeralds, etc?

8. Have I used 'male' imagery for the hero and female for the heroine?

9. Have I used the weather/heat/cold to enhance and add to the atmosphere?

10. Have I considered the effect that the particular setting I have used will have on the state of mind of the characters?

11. Have I made it plain 'where' in the characters' lives the story takes place?

12. Have I used anticipation and slow build up to create atmosphere?

Exercises

Something to think about

Before you can write about your characters' sensuality, you need to explore your own. If you have a partner to explore this with – then fine. But check that they don't mind you taking notes first!

What I want you to think about and investigate, are the things that you find sensual. It could be the fall of someone's hair, or their eyes, or the way they walk.

I have a thing about men's hands – and their forearms. A crisp white shirt or a battered denim one, pushed back to reveal long, firm hands and the strong bones and muscles always make me take a second look.

What things attract you? What would you notice in those all-important first four minutes? What scents do you like/dislike? What sorts of clothes? And what do you feel about people who wear particular sorts of clothes? Are you someone who thinks a sharp, designer suit is the most attractive thing a man can wear? Or do you prefer a more rugged leather jacket and jeans and think that along with a suit comes an uptight personality?

List your feelings:

► The way some things make you think and feel.
► The clothes and colours you love – and the ones you hate.
► The touch that makes you shiver in sensual response.
► The one that turns your stomach in a totally different way.

And then look into how different settings might affect you.

► Do you love the heat of the sun and can't get enough of it? Or do you hate feeling hot and sticky?

► Would you hide indoors if it started to snow or pour with rain? Or would you be out there, making snowballs or splashing through puddles?

Think about places you have visited and loved – or the opposite. What sights, sounds, scents, flowers, colours, etc, spoke to you of the essential nature of that place? If you were spending your first four minutes there what would you notice?

Something to write about

Your writing task is to write some descriptions of people and places. Try to incorporate as much sensual detail as possible – and I'm not just talking about physical details – put in the way they speak, their laughter, a movement and so on.

Remembering those first four minutes, try to imagine how it feels to meet someone – the things you first noticed about them and the impressions those things gave you about the person you were looking at. Were they good or bad? Appealing or repellent? And how did those feelings change as you got to know them?

Try to write a first meeting between two central characters – your hero and heroine in two ways.

1. When the hero and heroine are meeting for the very first time, never having seen each other in their lives before.

2. When they are meeting up again after a time apart – months, or years – you decide.

Then put those two people into two very different settings and show how where they are affects the way they feel and the situation between them.

Once you have that sensuality clear in your mind, we'll take it one stage further – and move on to passion.

7

Passion

What is passion in a romance?

Firstly, let's make one thing clear. Passion is not just sexual passion. If we consult the dictionary again – passion has these definitions:

> 'strong feeling or agitation of mind, especially rage, often sorrow; a fit of such feeling, especially rage; an expression or outburst of such feeling; ardent love; sexual desire; an enthusiastic interest or direction of the mind; the object of such a feeling.'

Perhaps you'll see why we looked at emotion at the beginning of this book, and have only just got round to passion. This is the reason I write Modern Romance (Presents). It has nothing at all to do with the amount of love-making, explicit or otherwise, my hero and heroine indulge in, but the amount of **emotion, intensity** and **passion** that I can bring into a book.

My characters get very intense about things. They feel deeply, rush into anger, agonise over hurts, see insults in things, react sharply. They are very, very passionate people. Their lives during the story are full of passion, tension, intensity, emotion. So if they're deeply involved in anything, whether it's eating or arguing, joking or loving, they experience it as something so sharp and clear it's almost painful.

And that includes each other – which will inevitably lead to love-making. Because, let's face it – no matter how far you personally want to go with describing the actual act of love-making – whether you want to go into great sensual detail or shut it all away behind a bedroom door – no one is ever going to believe that a couple are made for each other, that they're headed for a happy-ever-after ending – if there is no vital passionate spark between them.

Sex is a vital part of any relationship and you need to show at least the seeds of it in your characters' reactions to each other.

Writing love scenes

I've been told I write good love scenes – but I don't find them easy. After all, there is only so much variety you can manage. Sometimes I feel like writing – 'Okay, you all know what happens here – so use your imagination!'

But I have to write them – and I think that, certainly in Modern Romance, they're a very important part of the development of the relationship – so what do I do to get the right 'feel'?

The first thing you have to consider before you even start writing is, what are you comfortable with?

Comfort levels

Your reading of various different lines in the romance genre will have shown you that there are many different levels of sexuality in the books. It varies not only from line to line, but also from author to author within a line. You need to consider which one of these you are most comfortable with. The comfort level matters for both the reader and the writer.

For the reader

When a reader picks a series book from the shelves, she will usually know according to the line and author what level of sexuality she will be reading. Series writers meet readers' expectations. If the reader is comfortable with that level of sensuality, she will probably pick up that line or that author again.

For the author

Comfortability for you as an author is also important to your story and your writing, whether you write sweet love scenes or steamy ones.

You might want to choose the line to write for according to how much you enjoy or don't enjoy writing love scenes. I say that because love scenes, and the sensuality that goes with them, don't begin or end on specific pages of a book. They pervade the entire book. The perspective, the sensuality, the depth of emotion shouldn't be any different in your love scenes than they are in the rest of the romance. If anything, they should be heightened. You can't take sensuality in and out of a book like a spare part. It's either an aspect of a writer's voice or it's not and that is why the previous chapter was devoted to this subject. You may be able to add or delete actual love scenes, but you won't be able to erase the sensual and passionate tone of the overall book.

If you don't enjoy reading hot, steamy books, chances are you won't enjoy writing them. If you don't enjoy reading a 'sweeter' romance because it doesn't have the intensity of mood and passion that you are looking for, then the chances are you won't find writing one a satisfying experience. And if you don't enjoy sensual scenes, or believe in the reasons for their being in a book, then it will show in your writing. Love scenes, like the rest of a romance, are more than mechanically written scenes with all the right elements. They should be scenes teeming with emotion, tension and intensity in addition to writing skill. And if you don't feel it, how can you write it?

You are writing as your characters

The other important point to remember when you are writing love scenes is that you are not writing for yourself. You are writing scenes that explore your hero's and heroine's fantasies – not yours.

When writing a love scene, you need to forget about who will read this book, and not worry about your mother reading it or your husband, or your great aunt. Readers who think that what they're reading is your fantasy will be wrong.

You should write what suits your characters. It's their story you're telling after all.

Before and after

The most important things to remember when writing a love scene are not what actually happens within the scene itself. The moment that your hero and heroine come together intimately can be thrilling and erotic or it can fall as flat as unrisen bread. This is because it is not the love-making that creates the excitement. As with the plot in which the love scene appears, it is the tension and the emotion that build up to it, and the changes in the characters' behaviour, in their relationship that results from it which will stay in the reader's mind.

So when you are creating a love scene, what you need to remember and emphasise are:

▶ What happens **before**. What precedes the scene, the emotional and sexual tension that leads up to it?

And

▶ What follows **afterwards**. What results from the scene? What emotional changes in the characters and their relationship with each other follow from it?

A love scene must always have a purpose

The next important element in writing love scenes is purpose. Apart from the obvious answer that a love scene needs to be in a romance because sex is a vital part of any romantic relationship between two people, it needs to have a reason for being there within this book.

You need to ask yourself:

▶ Why is it there?
▶ What will it reveal?
▶ What will it tell you about the characters?
▶ How will it change the hero's and heroine's relationship?
▶ How will it move the plot along?

Why put love scenes in a book at all?

Naked bodies breed honesty. They also change the relationship once and for all. You can never go back to how it used to be – and neither can your characters.

Besides trust, a love story revolves around sharing intimacy. Romances are about two people who are attracted, then fall in love by getting to know each other. They want to know each other's minds, hearts, and souls, and the physical knowing that goes with it. That's why love scenes are an integral part of romances.

It isn't just a matter of the right body parts in the right places without the commitment and emotion. Purpose is all-important when writing a love scene. Ask yourself:

▶ What is the purpose of your love scene?

▶ How is it essential to this story?

▶ Why can't you delete it?

▶ Is it a coming together in the heat of passion that the hero and heroine will regret?

▶ Is it a generous and mutual giving and taking – true sharing?

▶ Is the heroine thankful the hero rescued her from a dangerous situation?

▶ Does the love scene break down the barriers around a hero's or heroine's heart?

▶ Does it bring the hero and heroine closer or push them apart?

▶ What does it change permanently and irrevocably in the relationship?

Building towards a love scene

Sexual tension in writing a romance is a crucial element combined with emotional tension. But this tension does not result from stopping the characters from consummating their physical relationship by using interruptions, ringing telephones, knocks at the door, changes of heart, and other things. True sexual tension builds through a difference in tone, subtlety, and progression of sensuality throughout the entire book.

A love scene is not just the act of intercourse. It builds up through each moment that the hero and heroine are together. The first time a hero and heroine consciously touch, the first time they kiss, are love scenes. Love scenes are always a challenge; there is so much about them that is always the same. But each time you write one you need to ask yourself:

▶ How can I make this love scene unique *for this couple?*
▶ What will make this one different?
▶ What will make this one work?
▶ How do I make it personal to them?

And it's not a matter of where the couple are, where he puts his hand, or where she kisses him.

It has to do with emotion – the emotion that happens before, the emotion that happens during, and the emotion that happens after.

Just as the moods of the love-making are not the same from book to book, from character to character, then the words you use for that emotion are not the same.

So how can you make each scene as individual as possible?

Uniqueness of imagery

This brings us to the next important element in writing a love scene.

Uniqueness

How can a kiss, for example, be unique to a couple? How will a touch feel to these particular people? How would they describe what they can see, hear and feel?

Imagery is important. Your images can be as unique as your hero and heroine. They have to come from the couple, their background, the setting. If you are inside your hero or heroine's mind, seeing everything from their viewpoint, then you will use the sort of images that person would use in their own thoughts.

▶ A sailor will think of the sea.
▶ A dress designer will think in terms of satins and silks and other fabrics.
▶ An artist might think of oils or watercolours.

The images are not the ones that would work for you. They have to be unique to this couple.

Creating sexual tension

Why is sexual tension so important? Because the heat, the intensity of a book, the steaminess of the sensuality doesn't necessarily have anything to do with the consummation scene but rather with the characters, and the emotional (that word again) relationship between them.

Once they've 'done it', once they've made love, there will be an inevitable let down – both for them and the reader. At this point, all tension could seep away from the book, leaving it limp and lifeless. The tension continues with the conflict.

You might want to look back at the chapter on conflict again. Because conflict is important in creating and maintaining sexual tension, each scene you plan should be propelled by the conflict and that includes the love scenes. To begin page one with the sexual and emotional tension that will invade every scene, you need a defined conflict. Without it, the plot limps along with no strength and you end up with a series of disconnected scenes, and the love scenes have no real impact or importance. Love scenes have to be more than a list of what's happening physically. They have to draw in and from every nuance of character and conflict that has preceded the scene and will come after.

Each love scene should connect to the conflict in some way because although these two people want to be together, for some reason they are also being torn apart. That tension is there through every scene; tightening the muscles, stretching the nerves, putting a double edge on each move and event.

This will add to that emotional punch you are trying to create, both for each scene and the whole book, and it will generate that PTQ, making the reader turn the pages faster and faster.

Timing and its effect

How soon in your romance does the first 'big' love scene happen? In manuscripts I read by beginners, it often happens too soon. This is because they believe that love-making scenes are what create intensity and passion in a story, when in fact it is the intensity and passion that build to create the sexual tension.

You can use a stunning kiss to establish sexual tension early. But use kisses wisely. Even a first kiss can happen too soon. I like to build the tension until the reader is ready to explode with frustration. Then when the kiss comes, or the first love scene happens, the reader savours it more.

This again is where that conflict is important – if the conflict isn't dealt with then the tension remains. And if that tension remains between your two characters, then you don't have true intimacy.

There are two very different types of intimacy:

▶ physical, and
▶ mental.

You can be physically intimate with someone, have had sex with them, without ever being truly mentally and emotionally intimate with them. And you can be mentally intimate with someone on the deepest level of friendship without ever having been physically intimate.

But you can't really fall in love without being emotionally intimate. And a romance is the story of your hero and heroine finding that emotional intimacy and so falling in love.

Often the hero and heroine 'know' each other in the Biblical sense – but they don't *know* each other. Not truly, not totally, not real, deep, heartfelt, intimate knowing and trusting the other person.

After the first consummated love scene, the dynamics of the relationship between hero and heroine changes. This affects plotting. When two people make love, they are changed and this is reflected in the remainder of the plot line, in the way your characters think, and most of all in the way they act around each other. They are more likely to touch freely, to be more familiar, freer to express their thoughts, more free to share. There is a deepening of the relationship that goes beyond the physical.

From now on, everything that happens will have more of an impact. It will mean much more than ever before. A kindness will be enhanced, a betrayal will hurt much more, a lie will devastate.

And conflict will seem so much worse.

Don't waste this. Don't lose the added tension, the extra emotion that love-making between your characters will create. A love scene is about so much more than just physical intimacy.

Character and growth

In love scenes, you must be faithful to your characters but you can let them grow. For instance, if your heroine is shy and reserved, can she be a tigress in bed? Your characters must be consistent and some of the shyness is sure to show before and after. But in trusting she can become free. Once she is, she will not be the same shy, reserved person. Something about her will change. In like manner if the hero is withdrawn, he will not suddenly blurt out all his feelings after the first love scene. He might blurt out one—or consciously decide to share one. But as he gets to know the heroine and becomes more intimate with her, he will change too.

Aftermath – where do they go from here?

To me what really matters in a love scene is the 'before' and 'after'. That is where that most important of all the senses – the mind – comes in.

What really helps me write a love scene is the way that I've built up to it. The events that have happened before this development – the mood of the moments before and the way that this has moved into the couple making love. I try to make each love scene different and to make sure that each one moves the relationship along.

Never forget the 'after' as well as the 'before' and the 'during'. To me, a love scene isn't just put in to show the physical passion between these two people or to create a sensual atmosphere. In the course of the story you need to show how that moment of intimacy changed things between them – made them feel more secure, or totally lost. Whether it convinced her that he loves her – or quite the opposite. How will they feel 'the morning after' – or whenever the passion recedes and they have to face each other again? Because love-making strips humans naked. They reveal so much more than their bodies to each other – and if the scenes before give you the build up to the love-making scene, then the moments after are what will lead you into the next stage of your story and the next stage in the development of their relationship.

Finally, there are no rules about when, how soon in the book, the story or the relationship, or how many love scenes you need/can put in/must put in. Leave it up to your characters to tell you. As I said before, there is often more tension in anticipation than actual fulfilment. You need to build up the sensual atmosphere all the way through – a touch, a look, a scent – it's like a wonderful piece of music, working up to a huge crescendo. Go with the flow – think what your characters are feeling – and write what you feel comfortable with.

Using the five senses

So how do you write a love scene? You want to think of all the senses and bring them into play. And you want to visualise the scene as vividly as possible.

▶ Where are your hero and heroine:
  – somewhere cold or somewhere hot and humid
  – on a bed with satin sheets or perhaps the rougher feel of a carpet
  – or perhaps they are outside or in a barn full of hay?
  – Maybe there is a real fire. Imagine the warmth of the flames and the flickering, changing light playing over the pallor of skin, shadowing faces.

▶ What scents are there:
  – your heroine's perfume
  – the tang of pine wood on a fire?
  – Or maybe even the fresh scent of crushed grass if it's that outdoor scene.

▶ What can they taste:
  – what have they eaten or drunk
  – could your heroine taste coffee or brandy on his lips?
  – Maybe she has just cleaned her teeth so her mouth is clean and fresh and minty.

▶ What can they see:
  – those flames again or is the room totally dark
  – is the sun blazing down on them?
  – would your heroine close her eyes so that not seeing could make her feel things all the more intensely?

▶ Then of course there's the all-important touch.
  – Is it gentle, tentative, delicate and stroking or urgent, demanding, fast maybe even at times a little harsh?

▶ What sort of sounds will be heard:
  – the sounds of breath, gasps or sighs
  – the mutter of voices?

Using dialogue in love scenes

Dialogue can be tricky in a love scene, because very often people don't actually talk. Or when they do, it will be in half-broken phrases, choked off words – because in love-making I don't think anyone speaks in neat, precise and complete sentences. Sometimes the things people say will sound banal, even silly, at other times, but if you get the pacing right then it will seem right.

Try to introduce some sort of dialogue into a scene so that you can make your reader see and hear the scene (showing not telling). Also dialogue will keep the pace moving. So even if it's just your characters muttering each others' name or gasping 'Yes' in encouragement, it will make the scene all the more vivid because of it.

On the other hand, I have never found it believable or convincing if the hero – or, equally, the heroine, starts to go into rhapsodies of delight over their partner's skin, hair, breasts, eyes. . . whatever. There is a fine line between the erotic and the laughable so try to be aware of it.

Mood and pace

You will also need to consider the mood of the scene you are writing so that you can pace the scene to fit it.

Mood

▶ Is this a scene of sex following on from anger – from some huge row that has had your characters blazing at each other in fury before it turns to equally blazing sensuality?

▶ Or is it slow, gentle, secure, confident love-making when they know each other and are happy in each other's arms?

▶ Has the build-up been one of laughter, teasing, so that they are still smiling as they kiss?

▶ Or is the atmosphere tense and fearful, so that they are huddling together for support and protection?

▶ Who is the seducer and who is seduced?

Because angry sex is very different from slow, gentle, giving sex, you need to look at the scene as it builds.

▶ What is happening between your hero and heroine just before?

▶ What mood are they in with each other?

▶ Are they both totally involved or is one of them fighting their feelings like mad?

▶ Are they happy and confident together or is there a lack of trust that would put a sharp edge of unhappiness onto the wonderful physical feelings?

Each one of these moods will result in a totally different sort of pace.

Pacing

▶ Are your characters building slowly, slowly to a height or rushing into bed in desperate hunger?

▶ Will they delay certain moments and draw out other ones?

▶ Is this a long, slow, love-making, one where they know each other well and know just where to touch and how to get a response?

▶ Or is it a fast, urgent, greedily snatched voyage of discovery – where they feel they just can't get enough of each other fast enough?

A modern woman

Yet another of those popular myths about romances is that the heroine must be sweet, innocent, virginal and downright naïve. This is no longer the case even in historical romances. The way she behaves in the bedroom will depend on the sort of heroine you have created – her age, her background, and her experience. But I think editors want to see a woman who is a match for the hero. She may have been married, or had other lovers; she may have a child. Or she may still be a virgin through choice.

But she will also match up to her hero. She will not be passive. She may not be aggressive, but she will want to pleasure as much as be pleasured. In contemporary romances the hero and heroine are equals and the love scenes and their interplay will eventually reflect that.

Most of all remember that your hero and heroine must be real to the reader for the love scene (like the rest of your novel) to work. If the reader is totally involved in the characters' lives and emotions, the love scenes will flow and the reader will believe in them and find them as emotionally appealing as the rest of the book.

The hero – and safe sex

Remember that your hero must act like a hero. He should always show personal and moral integrity even through anger when he has good reason to be angry. He can be aggressive, but never abusive.

Another point that needs to be considered is that in today's society, it would not be considered very heroic if a man – or his heroine – did not consider the essentials of protection against unwanted pregnancy, AIDS, or other sexually transmitted diseases. Now, much more than ever before, a romance writer has to include the use of condoms and other forms of birth control.

And here is another issue where writing romance in the 21st century has been affected by changes in society of the time. If a hero is seriously responsible and conscientious about using contraception, the possibility of an unplanned pregnancy fades rapidly – and with it the chance of one of those favourite Secret Baby plots. So you need to find a balance between total irresponsibility and getting carried away in passion so that at this one particular moment such considerations were forgotten.

Again, it's another reason for getting right inside your characters and understanding their thoughts and motivation.

How far can you go?

How far can you go with love scenes?

The first thing that you will have to remember are the levels of sensuality within the line that you have chosen. And this can only be judged by attentive reading.

Always remember that you are writing *romance* not erotica and definitely not pornography. The emotional content of the book must always have the most emphasis in what you are writing.

Without getting graphic, in a steamy book you can go as far as your imagination, experience, love, commitment and a caring relationship can take you.

Using the right language

Finally, we need to consider another aspect of the language you would use within a love scene. You want to write using language that is sensual, rich, evocative and in character for your hero and heroine. But you will also want to think about the words you use for the body parts involved. Here are some terms that have been used – how would you react to reading them in a love scene?

▶ proud shaft
▶ manroot

▶ erection
▶ penis
▶ rosy peaked mounds
▶ burgeoning breasts
▶ creamy globes.

In a romance you don't want to be too graphic, but equally you don't want to use euphemisms that have the opposite effect to what you plan. You want to build up a sensuous, passionate atmosphere so beware of using words that do no more than make your reader giggle. Think about some of the euphemisms that can be used and try to make sure that you aren't creating an unplanned comic effect.

12 questions about passion

1. Am I writing with the degree of sensuality that I am personally comfortable with? And am I happy to put this scene in here now and because it should be there?

2. Am I writing at a level of sexuality that is appropriate to the line I am writing for?

3. Have I 'got rid of my mother' so that I can write freely – i.e. for myself and no one else?

4. Have I considered the mood of the scene and written the sex accordingly?

5. Have I used all five senses?

6. Have I used details appropriate to the period – clothing, setting, likelihood?

7. Have I considered the importance of 'safe sex', responsible hero, birth control?

8. Have I made my characters act in character – and react in character?

9. Have I taken into account *where* the scene takes place – and how that will affect it?

10. Have I taken into account where in the characters' development – and where in the book this takes place?

11. Have I written about before and after?

12. Have I developed the changes that must result from this scene?

Exercises

Something to think about

What I want you to think about is the love scenes that you have read in books (or seen in films or on TV if that helps). Think about the scenes you've read that stay with you; the ones you think worked on all levels; the ones you loved; the ones you felt were passionate – or warm – or tender.

▶ Which authors do you think write 'love-making scenes' as opposed to 'steamy sex'?

▶ Which ones embarrass you – and why?

▶ Which ones seem pale and insipid – or just right?

You're looking at what you feel comfortable reading and what you enjoy reading. That's what you'll enjoy writing. If you feel yourself blushing all over while just reading, you'll never be comfortable trying to write it.

But don't just look at the actual sexual moments – look at the build up to the scene – the emotions the couple are feeling – the mood they're in. The reasons *why* they get into bed (or wherever!) at that point. It isn't always just because of the obvious reasons.

In other words – what makes the sort of love scene you want to read – and so to write?

Something to write about

Write a love scene.

Take the conflicts and emotions you've already thought of. Add in some of that sensuality and the dialogue – inject it with the essential passion – then light the blue touchpaper and stand well back. And then do it again.

Why do it again?

What I want is for you to look at the same sort of scene in very different moods and atmospheres and situations. Think about:

▶ *Where* – where are your hero and heroine at this time?

▶ *When* – when in the relationship? When in the story? When in their lives?

▶ *Why* will they make love now and not earlier or later?

▶ *What* mood are they in?

Write it from a tender, warm, gentle viewpoint. Or one where they are angry with each other. How would it be different if they've only just met? Or if they knew each other before and have met up again after a long time?

- ▶ How would that affect the *pace* of the scene?
- ▶ Use all the five senses.
- ▶ Add in some dialogue.

And don't forget that essential before and after. Don't just fade out on a line like 'And all the world exploded into stars. . .' What happens next?

8

Heroes

Do I need to tell you why heroes are important? I shouldn't think I do. But just to remind you – it's romance that we're writing. Romance is the developing relationship between a man and a woman. Without a hero there is no romance, no relationship.

The reader may put herself into the place of the heroine, but it's the hero she remembers. The hero she falls in love with. So really, although the heroine is vital (and we'll come to her next) – it's the hero who carries the book, especially in a line like Modern Romance (Presents).

What makes a hero?

Heroes are easy – aren't they? If you've got a tall, dark, handsome man, a name like Luca or Vincenzo or Hassan or Nick, you're away. If he is successful, rich, powerful and dynamic too, what more do you need? You need *lots* of other things too, such as: believability, motivation, feelings, a past, a life, relationships, passions, family, etc.

I have read far too many would-be-published novels in which the poor hero becomes a sort of cardboard figure striding around the place, sneering, seducing and tossing the heroine aside – and then at the last minute he declares his love for her and they fall into each other's arms and live happily ever after. Hmmmm! That really isn't going to work. No modern reader is going to believe it for a start.

The Alpha male

I write Modern Romance/Presents and the Presents hero is Alpha male – that means he is rich, powerful, successful, dominant, forceful, gorgeous.

Sandra Marton likens the Alpha male to the Alpha wolf – the powerful, proud leader of the pack. The Alpha is the tough guy hero, James Bond, Mr Darcy in *Pride and Prejudice*, Mr Rochester in *Jane Eyre*, Rhett Butler in *Gone With the Wind*.

The **Alpha hero** is:

▶ A leader.

▶ Macho with a heart of gold.

▶ Handsome in a strong, ruggedly masculine way.

▶ Powerful and successful.

▶ He's strong, determined, driven, and he can be totally ruthless when the situation calls for it.

▶ He is such a strong, forceful personality that this can make him the sort of man you – and his heroine – either love or hate.

But there is also the less macho, gentler, more sensitive type of hero. Romance writers call this hero the Beta hero.

The Beta hero

The **Beta hero** is:

▶ No less successful, masculine and handsome than the Alpha hero, but in a softer version.

▶ He is more playful and relaxed.

▶ Charming.

▶ More of the 'boy (or man) next door' type.

▶ Less of a fantasy than the Alpha hero.

▶ More considerate of his heroine's feelings and opinions.

▶ He is the sort of man that a reader can actually imagine meeting, falling in love with, marrying – and being able to live with!

There have been some wonderful, gentle, loving heroes – but please remember that when you're writing only a short romance, there is a very fine line between 'nice guy' and 'wimp'. Why do you think that all the soap operas deal with troubled relationships, difficult husbands, unhappy marriages? It's because, much as we all want it for ourselves – once the marriage settles down into that happy ever after ending, it is inevitably less interesting. The doubt, the uncertainty, the sharp edge isn't there quite so strongly any more.

And it's that sharp edge that gives a romance its emotion and the conflict. So if you want to have a more 'Beta' hero – make sure you give him a quiet strength. Make him his own man – with his own beliefs – and some very human limits. As we'll see when we look at 'vital vulnerability' (page 78) paragons of virtue – perfect people – are not always totally appealing.

The man behind the fantasy

Let's deal with that 'rich, successful, multi-billionaire, owner of corporations' hero type.

The first thing you must remember is that these are just *trappings*. They are 'props' – much like the things given to any actor in a stage play. For example, James Bond has his Aston Martin, his 'shaken not stirred' phrase, his sophisticated clothes, etc to give him the right image. But if you are creating a hero, you need to create a man who, if stripped of all those trappings, would underneath still be a man with hero ideals – generous, brave, strong, faithful... add whatever you want.

What else goes to make a hero? Gorgeous – that's usually taken for a given – but while 'tall, dark and handsome' is really just shorthand for 'She fancied him like mad' remember that 'tall, dark and handsome' can have very different meanings for different people.

Look back at the notes on sensuality and your own thoughts on what appeals to you. Did you put in anything about height? Or did you just put a non-specific 'tall'?

That 'tall' can mean so many different things. Someone who is 5′ 9″, like me, when they read the word 'tall' thinks 6′ plus – but someone like a friend of mine who is 4′ 11″ – and a half (that half inch is very important to her!) sees her husband who is 5′ 10″ as tall.

So it's all relative – as is 'handsome' – one woman's handsome is another's downright ugly, or way too pretty.

The important thing about this is that your hero is gorgeous *to his heroine* (and vice versa – we'll come back to this in the next chapter). As I mentioned, I had a scarred hero in *Fiancée By Mistake* – and the hero in *Marrying the Major* that I talked about earlier also had bad battle scars. But in the end a heroine won't see those scars – or a limp – or whatever. The man she loves is the man she loves and that's it.

The 'cruel' hero

Heroes are monsters, too, aren't they? That seems to be the general opinion. Heroes, particularly Modern/Presents heroes, come from the 'treat 'em mean, keep 'em keen' school of thought.

At times it can seem like that. The conflict in a book can work best – and so the emotional punch increases – when the hero appears to be, if not the total villain, then at the very least strongly ambiguous in his attitude to the heroine. He has to remain largely a mystery to her. She doesn't know how he feels about her, or why he is behaving in a particular sort of way. So she doesn't understand why he is behaving unpleasantly, even cruelly towards her.

But you, as his author – *must know*!

If you are going to give your hero some pretty tough – even some downright nasty things to do – then you *must have a very good reason for doing so.*

You must have him believing things that he can later find to be wrong, or acting on faulty information, or being blinded by his own prejudices. He can't just be cruel for cruelty's sake and because it makes a more tense and emotional story.

The hero's point of view

This is one of the reasons why so many authors now like to write in the hero's point of view. If the reader can see inside the hero's head, then she can see just why he is doing something, what wrong conclusions he's jumping to, what distorted beliefs he has. And so she can understand why this is happening.

For example, in my book, *The Hostage Bride* (Modern Romance 2001) the hero kidnaps the heroine – taking her away from her own wedding, just as she's setting out for the church. Now this could be a very dark, dangerous scenario, and for a time the heroine thinks so too. But he has his reasons and to him they are valid and important. And glimpses into his point of view show that. The reader has some clues into why he is behaving the way he is and so can start to understand and sympathise even when he seems to be behaving at his worst.

So when you give your hero that ambiguity, make sure you give him an explanation for it too. Show the past hurts, the misinformation, the distorted thinking that is making him make the mistakes. Don't just let him behave badly, 'because that's what heroes do' – it isn't! And no 21st-century woman is going to stand for it.

It's not just the heroine's love story

Just as you must show the way that your heroine is falling head over heels in love with the hero, so you must also show the same thing happening to him. If he starts off angry and cold, with his heart totally set against his heroine, there must be a slow, gradual thaw, moments when he slips from being icily distant into growing warmer and closer, until in the end he realises he can't live without her.

There are no rules for when the hero will find out how he really feels – but again you must have very good reasons why he doesn't say so. In *The Sicilian's Wife* for example, the hero has been in love with the heroine for years. And he is in love with her right at the opening of the book. In fact he's going to ask her to marry him. But then things change – and as they change, then he has first one reason then another for not telling her how he feels.

So as I always say, the 'when' isn't as important as the 'why'.

▶ Why does he know that now he loves her?
▶ Why does he not tell her?

Or if he does tell her why does she not tell him she loves him in return and fall into his arms and they walk into a happy ever after?

We're back to conflict again.

Heroes and emotion

Your hero may be a tough, macho type, but there is also plenty of scope for him to show his feelings – even if he doesn't ever want to talk about them! And anger and lust aren't going to be the only ones he ever shows.

I've made my heroes cry – not great breaking down, heaving sobs, but definitely tears in their eyes, moistening cheeks, clogging eyelashes into dark spikes – that sort of thing. Because I've had heroes whose wife/brother/unborn child has died – so they would be desperately hurt and not always able to hide it.

And if you have 'positive tears' – being overwhelmed with love so that emotion won't be controlled then that would work too. As the editors say so very often:

It's all in the execution.

You want to make sure he's a strong man expressing strong emotion – and it's not just Latin men who are like that.

Humour is also very attractive in a man and moments of laughter, gentle teasing or just lightening the atmosphere are wonderful contrasts to the emotional intensity that keeps your reader hooked. One of the Tender (Romance in USA) writers who has a wonderful touch with humour is Liz Fielding.

Avoiding stereotypes

One of the problems with creating one of the very popular Mediterranean, or Sheikh characters as a hero is that with such a short book, there is a danger of creating a stereotype – a hot-blooded Italian lover, an arrogant Sheikh, a proud Greek. There is also the belief that *only* Latin lovers are acceptable for some of the lines – notably Modern/Presents. But the truth is that if your manuscript doesn't work, changing your hero into a Greek tycoon, just because they are so popular, is not the way to guarantee success.

Your reader is looking for a particular type of hero when she chooses a Latin lover book, and basically that is the sort of man who is not a 'stiff upper lip' Englishman or a reticent (about emotions) American. She is looking for a hot-blooded, hot-tempered, passionate and powerful man. She expects a book with a lot of emotion and that is usually what she gets.

How do you avoid the stereotype trap? You remember that your hero is 'just a man' – and that's the real way to tackle this problem. Your hero may be a deeply unreformed, Alpha, Greek tycoon type – but that isn't *all* he is. It's what he is *other* than being a Greek tycoon that makes him a character first and then a hero. So yes, the Greek tycoon heroes will probably look very much the same, use the same smattering of Greek that the author knows, have the same pride, the same arrogance, etc that most Greek tycoons have – but it will be the background, the history that make him the essential *man* he is.

Your character will only appear as a stereotype if he is nothing *more* than just a tall, dark, swarthy, arrogant, wealthy cardboard cutout.

If he has a family, relationships, a past, values, ambitions, faults, weaknesses, vulnerability, passion... *that's* what makes him an individual and an individual is so much more than a stereotype. Then his Greek/Spanish/Italian/French characteristics become just that – characteristics – and not stereotypical elements.

I think you can use some aspects of stereotypes to great effect in short series romances. They are a way of 'shorthanding' things for readers who are very much at home in the genre and who know when you say 'Greek tycoon' you mean a certain sort of man.

But I think the whole point has to be that once the writer has said 'Greek tycoon' or 'Spanish count' or 'Outback cattleman' or whatever, to establish a foundation for the character, the really good books move on from there.

This is the way that the really good writers work. They take the Greek tycoon and they make him a particular man with a particular background and set of hopes and dreams and strengths and weaknesses and they set him apart from all the other Greek tycoons who have ever populated the Presents line. They make him memorable. They make him live in the hearts of readers as well as the heart of the heroine.

Vital vulnerability

Why is that vulnerability so vital – especially in a hero? Because perfection isn't totally appealing. It can be scary. It can be totally unbelievable. It can seem inhuman. It can be just *too much*.

When you are creating a hero and a heroine you want to create realistic people, people who will appeal to the readers, people who are believable and sympathetic so that the reader will relate to them. And that vulnerability will give more emphasis, more edge to the emotion and the conflict that make up the plot – it will also enhance the passion and deepen the characters of your hero and your heroine.

Why especially for the hero?

Vulnerability is even more important for the hero. Especially if you're dealing with an Alpha male.

As I've said, the Alpha male is strong and powerful and forceful and dynamic and successful . . . add in all the rest of it, the cars, the money, the looks, and then you have a romance hero. But at heart he's just a human being. Remember what I said about being able to strip away all the power and wealth, the trappings – and still be left with a core of a hero? Well that's what you're trying to show.

Readers can be blinded by the trappings. They can see the macho posturing and sneering, the forceful dynamism, the 'take control' attitude, and sometimes the apparent cruelty that is part of the hero's behaviour, and they can end up thinking that this is the *real* man. But remember that I said he had to have very good reasons for behaving as he does – well, then those reasons are part of his vulnerability.

What sort of vulnerability?
The sort of feelings that I'm talking about are:

▶ Feelings that go deep and have their roots in the past.

▶ Misinformation that leads him to make mistakes.

▶ Scars from past hurts that affect his judgement in the present.

▶ Lessons learned from other experiences that mirror what is happening in the present in this story.

If the hero is totally untouchable – how is he ever going to fall in love?

What is it about the heroine that touches something in him in a way that no one has ever done before?

What secret is he hiding, what dark memory, what pain, what betrayal, what disillusionment is he trying to hide?

There needs to be a chink in his armour – the reason why he's doing something – the soft inner heart that he's trying to protect – through which your heroine can reach him. In a word **motivation.**

But this will also gain reader sympathy and it will give the heroine a way to reach him. This is one of the reasons why the hero's point of view has become so popular in recent books. It gives the reader an insight into his thoughts and feelings, so that we can see that vulnerability in action, not just be told about it at the end when we have to assimilate it suddenly and believe that this is what has motivated him all the way through, in the same moment that we need to believe he has fallen in love.

Of course the vulnerability – and the obstacle to the two people coming together – can just be the fact that, particularly with the hero, he doesn't have the emotional vocabulary to communicate how he feels. There can be little that is more poignant than the struggle of a macho male to reach the woman he loves when he just doesn't know how to communicate his feelings to her. In these circumstances such men often hide behind even more macho posturing rather then admit their vulnerability – so right there you have a conflict around which your story can be based.

And that vulnerability will have your readers rooting for your characters and cheering them on.

12 questions about heroes

1. Have I created a hero with whom I can fall in love with and communicated the excitement he makes me feel?

2. Is my hero appropriate to the romance line that I am aiming for? If they are looking for an Alpha male do I find him sympathetic or so repellent that I can't write about him?

3. Have I given my hero a strong physical presence but avoided the 'tall, dark, handsome' cliché?

4. Does my hero have a past and a family and a life before he appears on page one, even if these don't necessarily ever appear in the book?

5. Does my hero have goals and hopes and dreams that drive him on?

6. If my hero has prejudices/flawed reasoning, hatreds, anger – have I given him good and justifiable reasons for these?

7. Have I given him strong motivation for his actions – no matter how good or bad?

8. Have I given believable reasons for my heroine to fall in love with him?

9. Have I given him his own patterns of speech or idiosyncrasies of language?

10. Does he have that 'vital vulnerability', that chink in his armour that will let the heroine reach him?

11. Have I given him good reasons for falling in love with his heroine?

12. Do I know him well enough to be able to say exactly how he would react in any given situation, no matter how unexpected?

Exercises

Something to think about

For this exercise your thinking needs to be in several parts. You're thinking about heroes – but you need to consider *what makes a hero* – for you. Look at it from these points of view.

Physical

We've touched on this in the sensuality topic. You can have some fun here. Find a magazine filled with celebrities or film stars – or just sit back and daydream.

Think who makes your pulse rate quicken, your heart flutter – *and why*. Is it in his eyes, his mouth – his hair? What can he not have?

At a recent Author Day, a group of successful romance writers all brainstormed the topic 'what can a hero *not* be?' We all felt we could still make 'heroic' a short man, a man who wore glasses, a bald man. But perhaps not someone with acne – or who smelled – but then again under certain circumstances...

Mental attitude

▶ What is 'heroic' in your mind?

▶ What makes you remember certain heroes and not others?

▶ Who were your heroes – fictional or fact – when you were growing up? How have they changed as you've grown older?

▶ Do you now quail inside in embarrassment – or are you true to them still?

▶ What makes you love one man and hate another? Are you someone who loves Heathcliff – or do you prefer Mr Rochester in *Jane Eyre*? Would you find Rhett Butler wonderful or a reprobate?

▶ Is your hero a white knight or someone with an ambiguous reputation and a tarnished past?

▶ Do you want the rough, tough, cowboy or investigator type – or the sophisticated, sleek, business tycoon in a designer suit?

What do you think a hero should **offer to his heroine***?*
It can't just be money and security for life – what's *really* important?

▶ Honesty?
▶ Faithfulness?
▶ Strength?
▶ Power?

Should he let her be independent or play the old-fashioned 'husband as supporter' role? Should he be:

▶ a poet
▶ a househusband
▶ a good father
▶ a great lover
▶ a powerful force in society?

Do you prefer the exotic foreign hero – and if so, from which countries? Or do you like your heroes 'home grown' – again, from which country – and why?

Something to write about

Create a hero to go with the conflict and the emotions you've been looking at.

▶ Give him a name – a hero has to have a good 'hero name' – a nationality, a job or a career – well, some source of income!

▶ Ask yourself questions about him – about his family – his relationships in the past etc.

▶ Write a description of him. This one's physical. A basic, 'first four minutes', just met him description. What would your heroine see when she first looks at him?

▶ Now try something different – get your heroine to tell someone about him – her mother, her sister, her best friend. Get her to say why she loves him (or why she hates him). What he does or says that makes her feel this way. Use most of what we've already looked at – emotion, conflict, sensuality, dialogue.

▶ And finally, get your hero to tell you about himself. Get him to say what's most important to him. Who *is* he really? What does he value? Who is he close to? Anything – so long as it builds up a picture of a real man. Give him his 'voice'.

Remember, this is a man to fall in love with. He doesn't always have to be conventional and a 'typical' hero. As long as you think he's wonderful and exciting and you can communicate that excitement to your reader you'll have a hero on your hands.

In the next chapter we'll look at a heroine for him.

9

Heroines

Character building

This is a section that applies to both the hero and the heroine, so I'm putting it in between the chapters on them to help you build up characters for both.

Strong, believable, appealing characters are the most important part of your book. They are the way to grab your reader's interest, win their sympathy, and get them involved in your story. All the twists and turns and complicated plots in the world won't redeem a book that is peopled by stiff, wooden, one-dimensional people. Your characters have to come alive in your reader's minds, and to do this you really have to *know* them inside out.

Asking questions

So how do you get to know your characters? You need to find out everything you can about them. Many would-be authors start out with a hero and a heroine who have a name, an age, a physical appearance, perhaps a job, and – well, that's it. They put these half-formed creatures into a plot – the plot they have decided on already – and then wonder why the plot doesn't work, the romance has no emotional punch and the conflict doesn't develop as it should.

And perhaps the next thing that happens is that they get terrible writer's block and they have no idea how to go any further or where to turn – and they abandon the book because it 'just doesn't work.'

The reason it just doesn't work is because the characters haven't come alive. If your characters are alive and vivid and feel like real people, then they will quite often take things out of their author's hands. They will start to dictate the action, take their creator on all sorts of twists and turns that she wasn't expecting – often ones that are so much better than she ever hoped for. In short, they will tell you their story and all you have to do is to write it down.

I always say that when I am writing a book, in my mind I see the characters come into my office, they sit down in a chair and start telling me about their relationship with the hero or heroine. I transcribe this onto my keyboard as they 'talk'. Occasionally I might need to say, 'Why did you do that?' or 'What were you feeling then?' and they usually answer me!

Yes, you knew writers were mad, didn't you? But I know so many friends who write novels – of all sorts – for a living, and most of them work like this. They talk about their characters 'speaking' to them, telling them the story, or their motivation, or their feelings – and that's they way it works best for almost all of them.

Several well-established, bestselling authors suggest a technique of 'interviewing' your characters. You ask them all sorts of questions, some of which may never come into the plot you are writing, but which will build up a picture of the person you are dealing with. You ask questions that are factual, personal, emotional, and when you have the answers to those questions, you feel the character come alive and you start to understand how they might react in any situation that you might put them in.

The characterisation worksheet on pages 86/87 covers some of the details you might want to know. This list is not totally comprehensive, there is plenty more you could go on and ask, but it will give you some idea of how to get to know your protagonists.

Do you need to use all this information in a book? No, you will probably find that a lot of it is not directly relevant. But putting characters into a book should be like introducing two people you know well to each other. You will have some ideas about how they will react together and you will understand if they form an instant rapport on some things and not on others. You need to know your characters as well as you can and then if a situation arises that you weren't expecting you will be able to say exactly what the hero or the heroine will do.

The five Ws of writing romance

There is a rhyme by Rudyard Kipling that sums up a lot of what you need to know about writing.

> I keep six honest serving-men
> (They taught me all I knew);
> Their names are What and Why and When
> And How and Where and Who
> > 'The Elephant Child', *The Just So Stories for Little Children*

We have dealt with 'where' when we discussed settings, 'what' and 'how' will be discussed in Plotting (Chapter 10), and 'why' has its own chapter (Chapter 11). Obviously, 'who' is the question for this chapter, because we are dealing with characters. But this is also when the other 'W' comes in – the question that asks:

When?
The answer to this seems obvious – so equally obviously, it isn't! Because 'when' has several different angles of approach.

When does this story take place?
If you're writing a contemporary romance, then it takes place in the 'present day'. If it's a historical romance it takes place in 1066 or 1385 or 1642 – or whenever you've decided to set it. Right? Yes – as far as it goes.

The following applies to present day and the historical romances too. You should always remember that you are writing about heroes and heroines who are appropriate to the climate of society of the day. For example – 1950/1960s heroes – and often heroines too – could smoke like chimneys and no one minded. It was seen as sophisticated rather than dangerous. My very first paperback hero in *Game of Hazard* (1986) smoked. I wouldn't let a hero do that now.

This 'when' also has repercussions for the love scenes. Years ago it was understood that a 'nice girl' would say no and that was that. These days, it can be harder to explain why a heroine says no than why she would say yes. And would you consider a man heroic if he didn't at least suggest using a condom?

There are all sorts of other things that modern science has changed – birth control – paternity tests. The suspicion a hero might have had a child that was/was not his could once have lasted throughout the book but can now be dealt with in one chapter.

Get your facts right
If you are working on a historical book, make sure you get your facts right! I have heard of would-be writers who have medieval knights worrying about germs or Mary Queen of Scots telling Boswell to get a maid to make him a sandwich.

You will need to make sure – particularly with reference to your heroine – that the things you want her to do were in fact possible, for a woman, in the period you've used for your book. You'll need to know what was acceptable and what was totally frowned on. This doesn't mean to say that you can't let your heroine rebel against the social dictates of the day – just that you must make sure that she is the sort of character who is capable of doing so, and of coping with the fallout if she does.

Whether your book is ultra-modern, a medical drama, set in the Second World War or in the Crusades – check your facts!

So that's the period aspect of it – next is the details of 'when'.

What season?
If your story is set in winter then you'll be writing about cold days, early nights, late dawns – summer in Greece might sound wonderful but could be almost too hot to do anything – spring in Scotland is not the same as spring in Cornwall. (American/Canadian/Australian readers can insert names of cities in the far North and the far South as appropriate). You don't want to set an outdoor seduction scene in the heather on the moors in January. You need to get your facts right – weather, flowers, crops, festivals, holidays etc. These can all be brought in to add to the colour and the reality of the story but only if you get them right.

What is this person's name?

Why was she or he named that?

What does she or he call themselves? Is there a nickname
or a variation on the name that she or he uses for
some people and not others? (As an example – think
about the different variations of Elizabeth that are
possible – Liz, Lizzy, Bet, Liza, Beth . . . Would
these make you think of different characters?)

Age? Birthday?

What does she or he look like?

Height

Build

Colouring – eyes – hair (what length? curly or
straight?)

Where (geographically) does she or he live?

Why did she or he choose to live there?

Do they live in a flat? A house? Or a narrow boat
on a canal?

Do they live alone? With others? Who?

What kind of car do they drive?

What are her/his most important material
possessions?

What are his/her hobbies?

What books/films/plays would they prefer?

What kind of music does he or she enjoy?

Do they have pets? Dog? Cat? Something
exotic?

What are his/her favourite foods and drinks?

What sort of education do they have? To
what level? Or was it in 'the university of life'?

What is his/her job?

Why did he or she want to do that job?

How do they feel about their work?

Who are her or his best friends?

How long have they known each other?

How would a friend describe her/him?

How does he or she feel about the opposite sex?

Why does he or she feel that way?

Is he or she married? Single? Widowed? Divorced?

Characterisation Worksheet

Was the divorce friendly or hostile?

Does he or she have children?

Does he or she have former lovers?

How would a former lover describe him/her?

How does he or she feel about love?

Has he or she ever been in love before?

How has that relationship affected them?

Who are his/her parents?

Where was he or she born and brought up – and in what circumstances?

What sort of a relationship does he or she have with parents?

Does he or she have brothers and sisters?

What is the relationship with them like?

How does he or she feel about himself?

Which one event in his/her life has made this person what they are today?

What achievement is he or she most proud of?

What trait does he or she have which they want to keep secret from the world?

What does he or she like most about his/her life?

What does he or she dislike most about his/her life?

What makes them most angry?

How does he or she behave when angry?

How would he or she behave if cornered?

How easy would he or she find it to admit that they were wrong?

What do they value most in all the world?

What is their most treasured possession?

How do they feel about money?

What would they never do – whatever the price?

What would this person die to defend?

What is his/her most likeable character trait?

What is his/her most troublesome or unlikeable character defect?

As the story begins, what crisis is he or she facing?

How will he or she react to it?

Why would he or she fall in love with the hero or heroine?

Why would the hero or heroine fall in love with them?

The weather affects people's personalities too. Some people want to hide away in winter and curl up by the fire. Others want to get out in the snow, to ski, to skate, to experience danger. Use this sort of 'when' to help reveal your characters' personalities as well as using it to colour a setting.

'When' in your characters' lives

Finally, when in your characters' lives is this story happening? It's often said that it's a good thing to start your story at a point of crisis in your hero or heroine's life. Say she's just lost her job or her fiancé has been unfaithful – or he finds he needs his estranged wife for some reason. So what has brought them to this present day in which they're living? What has happened either just immediately prior to this or in the distant past to make them the person they are?

Introducing reunions

And this is where the reunion question comes in. You'll remember that your characters aren't just born in the moment they appear on page one. They have past lives, past histories, past experiences, past lovers. Obviously this has all affected them and made them who they are.

The most evident of these is a story where your hero and heroine were together before the book starts – either married or just as lovers or even just friends. Then they have a past history to refer to – and usually to clear up and explain before they can move on in the present. But also people who have never met before bring their own personal baggage with them into any new relationship. You need to take that into consideration. It will affect their behaviour towards each other and towards events. It will leave them with scars, opinions, prejudices. It will leave them unwilling to do certain things and only too ready to plunge headlong into others.

Of course if your couple knew each other before, there are some things that will have changed and some things that will remain the same. You can use these both to emphasise and to change the conflicts that they had in the past – and its effect on the conflict they are dealing with now. A couple who were too young to cope with problems in the past might have matured enough to handle them now – another reason to consider when in your protagonists' lives your story is taking place.

When to tell your reader things

One more point – if your hero and heroine do have a past history – then you need to work on the balance of telling that back story and making sure that you focus on the present-day relationship. You will also need to decide whether your story works better by beginning in the present day and occasionally flashing back to the past or starting with the earlier stage of the relationship and then jumping to one/three/nine (or whatever) years later. Always remember that it is the present that the reader wants and don't overload them with the past.

Now we'll concentrate solely on the heroine.

The heroine

The heroine, even in these days of dual or more points of view, is the main filter through which the reader reads the story. As the reader is usually female herself (although not always) it is the heroine she allies herself with, whose focus she uses, whose feelings she experiences. It is the heroine's emotions that affect the reader strongly. So your heroine needs to be *sympathetic* to the reader.

Note – that's SYMpathetic – not *pathetic*. There are still too many myths around about the romance heroine, just as there are about the hero.

Myths

Sweet, innocent, very young, dependent, virginal, no job, no life, just passively waiting for the hero to come along and sweep her off her feet and live happily ever after with him.

Truth

You can go for all of the above if you think you can make it work – and it fits your plot – but these days you're far more likely to find a heroine who is anything that any modern woman can be. Of course this is for the contemporary romances – historical writers will need to watch the accuracy of how women were and how they lived in the period they've chosen. But for the best writers that doesn't limit them at all – they just make sure that they have justification for the characters they create.

Your heroine can be as feisty and independent as you want her to be. She can be conventional, unconventional(think of the wonderful Sierra with her purple hair in *The Inconvenient Bride*) free spirited, very young, very mature, sweet, bad-tempered, married, divorced, virginal, a single mother...

Realistic heroines

In short, if you are writing a 21st-century romance then your heroine should be a 21st century woman. And she should have a 21st-century response to any conflict that comes up.

Let me give you an example. I was once asked for an opinion on a novel in which the heroine went round to her boyfriend's (the hero's) flat and found another woman in his bed. The hero wasn't there – he was miles away – and the woman was his cousin. But instead of just asking him about it, the heroine ran away and they were separated for three years. When they met up again, there was another woman in the hero's life who claimed to the heroine that she had a relationship with the hero. So what did this 'modern' heroine do? Did she ask the hero what was going on? Did she talk about her fears? No – she ran away *again*. And this was supposed to be a woman of 26.

Now in my opinion, any 26-year-old today would tackle things very differently. My friends' daughters would just go straight in and tackle things – demand to know what was going on. They would need rather more than this flimsy evidence to make them turn and run.

So you need a heroine who is believable. She can be young and innocent if you like, even naïve, but if you want your reader to care about her – which you do – then please, no wimps, no doormats, no simpering sillies.

Let's have heroines that we can be proud of – heroines who are worthy of the heroes we create for them! You don't want a heroine who is just going to lie down and let the hero walk all over her. Where's the conflict in that? (Except in the mind of the reader who can't believe that she is reading this book!) Or the emotion – to me there's only one emotion in there and it's 'sad'. A heroine who stands up to the hero, gives as good as she gets, challenges him, makes him think, makes him fight for what he wants (or what he thinks he wants) – probably totally changing what he wants along the way – makes for good reading.

Vital vulnerability again

But don't make her too hard. The unsympathetic heroine can ruin a book. She doesn't have to be a saint either. That is why we come back to the term I've used before – vital vulnerability.

The reader wants to be able to identify with the heroine. A few believable flaws and some imperfections will make her more believable, someone they can identify with.

Many of the books open with the heroine at some point of crisis in her life. This is not just a hook, and part of the conflict, it's a way to leave her open to falling head over heels for the hero. And it also creates that vital vulnerability. If your heroine is going through life, totally happy, thoroughly fulfilled, no problems at all, not a worrying thought in her head – and she meets the hero and falls in love and he says he loves her and will she marry him and she says yes and they live happily ever after – it's not much of a story is it? Where's the conflict, where's the emotion?

But, you say, I'm using external conflict – the one that's imposed from outside. The one where someone else creates the problem – her family – her country – whatever. Fine. But if the heroine doesn't have this touch of vulnerability so that the conflict, wherever it comes from, doesn't affect her deeply, doesn't drag her in – then you have a story that is just a pale shadow of itself. A story that won't hit the reader in the face with the emotion it's capable of.

You can have your external conflict – but give the heroine some part of her character that this reaches into deeply and affects badly.

Give your heroine a life – past and present

Oh – and heroines don't just sit around waiting for Mr Right to come along and sweep them off their feet. They have lives, families, friends, careers. They might have had past lovers or husbands, they could have children.

In the same way that when you create a hero, you create a man who will still be heroic, even if you strip away the 'trappings' of wealth and power, so when you create a heroine, you create a woman who can handle what life brings by herself, who can be happy as she is, who isn't desperate for a husband to support her in the manner to which she'd like to become accustomed.

She doesn't *need* a man. But when the special one, the right one (the hero of course) comes along, he enhances her life to such an extent that she can't imagine it without him. It's a relationship of equals, co-pilots in life, not one proclaiming the paternalistic society where the heroine can't possibly manage without the support of a man.

An Alpha heroine for an Alpha male

In the last chapter we looked at the character of an Alpha male. This sort of man isn't going to find much satisfaction in a downtrodden wimp of a heroine. To continue the image of the Alpha wolf that Sandra Marton uses, the Alpha male needs an Alpha mate to cope with him, to match him and sometimes, when it's needed, to make sure he doesn't get away with too much.

The interest in romance is when two strong, determined personalities clash over something that is important to them. That is where the conflict comes from. To quote American author Jayne Ann Krentz:

> 'And the flat truth is that you don't get much of a challenge for a heroine from a sensitive, understanding, right-thinking 'modern' man who is part therapist, part best friend, and thoroughly tamed from the start. You don't get much of a challenge for her from a neurotic wimp or a good natured gentleman-saint who never reveals a core of steel.'

Therefore if you write the true romantic fantasy of a strong, forceful Alpha male meeting his match, then you need a very strong heroine because what she does is tame or at least 'domesticate' the hero. She can't do that if she's wishy-washy or a wimp or doesn't know her own mind. While she might not be strong in all areas and have to 'grow' just like he does – she still has to be strong enough to live on her own. She has to be capable enough to be attractive to him. He has to see her as someone he wants to *share* his life with – not someone he's just going to have to rescue over and over again.

Your novel can stand or fall on the character of your heroine. If your reader finds her unsympathetic, unbelievable, or downright incomprehensible, then a great deal of the interest and enjoyment in the book is lost and she is unlikely to want to finish the story, however great a plot you might have. But a sympathetic, interesting heroine, one the reader identifies with and cares about, will hold her attention to the very last page.

12 questions about heroines

1. Have I created a heroine who is appealing and sympathetic without being a wimp?

2. Is my heroine appropriate to the romance line that I am aiming for?

3. Have I given my heroine a strong physical presence and described her as an individual, not just the petite beautiful blonde innocent virgin of myth?

4. Does my heroine have a past and a family and a life before she appears on page one, even if these don't necessarily ever appear in the book?

5. Have I given my heroine an emotional and sexual past and thought about the way that will affect her behaviour in the present?

6. Does my heroine have goals and hopes and dreams that drive her on?

7. If my heroine has prejudices or flawed reasoning, hatreds and anger – have I given her good and justifiable reasons for these?

8. Have I given her strong motivation for her actions – no matter how good or bad?

9. Have I given believable reasons for my heroine to fall in love with the particular hero she is matched with?

10. Does my heroine have her own patterns of speech or idiosyncrasies of language?

11. Have I thought about the sort of job the heroine would do – and any ways, practical or emotional, in which it will affect her story and the development of the relationship in that story?

12. Have I given her hero good reasons for falling in love with his heroine? Can she cope with the type of hero he is?

Exercises

This time I want to give you this section in two parts.

1. I want you to go back to the section on the hero and the things to think and write about there. Do them again – but this time for the heroine. Create a heroine to match your hero, building up the picture for her as you did for him.

2. But now I want to add in something to think and write about that involves that vital vulnerability.

Something to think about
What I want you to do is to look at this topic in two ways:

▶ from the books that you've read
▶ from your own experience.

Think about books in which the hero (or the heroine) has done or said something that on the surface seems appalling. It looks as if it's cruel and hurtful and hateful – and yet when you discover their real reasons for doing it, you understand completely and see why they felt it was their only way out.

My own book *Hostage Bride*, has the hero kidnapping the heroine – but he felt it was the only way left open to him. This puts him in a *vulnerable* state of mind to start with – even if he doesn't show it to his heroine. And that vulnerability affects the way he behaves through the rest of the book.

Also think about things that may have happened in your own life. When you, or someone you know, might have said or done something cruel and hurtful – and the reasons why that happened. What was going on in your/their life at the time so that you/they weren't thinking straight? Perhaps you/they were really trying to say something else and it came out all wrong. Or perhaps the other person took it in totally the wrong way because of the way they were feeling.

Something to write about
Write a scene from your story – with the characters, the conflict etc that you've already been looking at. I want you to write this scene in three different ways.

1. Write it just as it is – basically report it – as an outside observer would see it – he came in and shouted at her – and she shouted back and he said. . .

2. Take one of the characters – either hero or heroine – and give their point of view on the scene – what was in their mind when they shouted, *why* they said what they did. What mood they were in. What had just happened to put them in that mood – and how they interpreted the other person's reactions to them. What they thought was going on in the other's mind.

3. Reverse this – so we get the other person's opinion of what's going on – their perspective – what they think is going on – and *why*.

10

Plotting

An original plot is hard to find

When I'm teaching, the students are usually stunned to find that plotting comes so late on the list of important points. When starting out as a writer, most people automatically think of putting the plot and how to create it first on their list of things to learn about. But I don't agree – for two reasons.

1. It is almost impossible to create any sort of truly original plot for a romance story. But you can create original characters.

2. When you are writing a romance, it is the *characters* who really matter. It's their emotional journey that makes the essential part of the plot, so you need to know your characters. Then put them together and that will often create the plot for you.

There is a theory in writing and literature that there are in fact only a limited number of plots – some say only seven – in the whole of the world of books. And if this is truly so, then the number of those plots suitable to be used as the core of a romance novel must be miniscule. Certainly there are some plots that appear again and again in romantic fiction. So the problem with writing a romance plot is not one of creating a totally new and different idea, but one of putting a new twist, a new spin on the old tried and tested stories that have been around for years.

Tried and tested plots

In romance writing there are plots that are so popular, and usually so successful, that over the years they have come to acquire titles all of their own. Writers now often refer to these titles to provide a quick summary of what their book is about. So you will hear someone saying 'It's a Secret Baby plot' and no more needs to be said.

Here are some examples of these sorts of plots:

▶ **The Secret Baby plot**
The hero and heroine have met before and been lovers in the past, but their relationship has broken up in bitterness and hostility. But when the heroine left, unknown to the hero she was pregnant with his child. Now the hero is back to find her – and will learn about his child – the 'secret baby'.

▶ **The Marriage of Convenience plot**
The heroine (it's usually the heroine) has a major problem, often a huge debt, that the hero can help solve. For his own reasons, he needs a wife, so he says that he will help her with her problem if she will marry him in a marriage of convenience. The marriage then turns into a real one.

▶ **The Amnesia plot**
The hero and heroine were married, or lovers, but as a result of some trauma or accident she – or sometimes he – has now lost the memory of their relationship. The plot centres around finding out what that relationship was truly like and why it broke up.

There are also other shorthand ways of describing basic plots, often by referring to the hero – a Sheikh book, a Cowboy, a Greek tycoon. These are just quick and easy ways to describe the 'hooks' in the plot so that they're understood quickly.

Using hooks effectively

'Hooks' in romance writing can take several forms:

▶ The use of a tried and tested plot that everyone will recognise and know what to anticipate.

▶ The use of certain set types of heroes who have been known to attract a large reading public – Greek Tycoons, Sheikhs, Cowboys or any Billionaire! In historical romances, Rakes and Lords, in medical romances Doctors and Surgeons.

▶ The use of certain themes that again have been used with great success in the past – revenge, amnesia, marriages of convenience, unexpected pregnancies.

▶ These themes then result in the use of 'buzzwords' – revenge, amnesia, bride, baby, marriage, mistress, passion, all of which shout the theme of the book or the hook in it to the browsing reader in a bookshop. You either like these titles or hate them. Unfortunately, they do add to the impression that the books are 'all the same'. But they make it very clear just what sort of a story it is. And as it is claimed that you have about ten seconds to attract a reader's attention and make them pick up a book, then this could be an advantage.

The problem with hooks is that some writers assume that all you have to do is to plan out a book with as many hooks as possible in it and you are guaranteed success. Here's another myth to rank along with the 'formula' one.

Hooks can be very successful. They are themes that have remained popular and intriguing over many years, appealing to many readers. The number of times that books with these sort of themes appear on the shelves is strong evidence to that fact. But this turns the hook into a double-edged sword. For every point in its favour because it is a familiar and tried and tested theme, there is one against it because many readers think, 'Oh no, not that story again!'.

Your use of a hook in your story can work or not – as the editors are always saying, 'It's all in the execution.'

Finding your voice

With a limited pool of potential plots for your romance, and with the hooks being so familiar already, how do you manage to create anything that is original?

You write using your own voice. This is an aspect of writing that many beginners find particularly difficult to grasp. They think you are just telling a story; recounting a series of events. You're just the narrator.

This is true, but a narrator has their own particular *style* of telling that story. And that is what you can bring to the story you are writing – the touch of individuality that lifts your book and makes an editor pay attention, even if you are telling the oldest story in the world.

How can you develop this elusive 'voice'? You need to do the following.

Read, read, read
It may sound ridiculous, even misleading, to tell you to read lots of other authors' works when you are trying to find your own individuality, but you need to recognise the different approaches that are possible.

One author may use a highly dramatised style, another may use humour, there are even some authors now who use first person in romance. Go back to the books you read and the notes you made in the first chapter of this book and see what you learned about the different voices of the authors you studied then.

Which one is most like you?
I'm not telling you to *copy* any established author's style. That's not what an editor is looking for. They already have, say a Kate Walker, or a Michelle Reid, or a Liz Fielding. But knowing which style is most like yours, and then looking at the type of story that they write, will help you define your own style as a writer.

Your style may not be the same as the one you admire
I can say this with feeling, as this is the trap I almost fell into when I first started out as a writer. I've always admired humour and wit, and several authors I most

admired and whose books I enjoyed could make me smile as I read them. But if I tried to write in that style, then I was lost. My characters aren't made for humorous writing. They don't take things lightly. On the contrary, they get very involved and intense about everything – so the writers I needed to look at were the ones who dealt with intensity, emotion and passion.

Your sort of words for your sort of story

When you've looked at the different styles and voices that other writers use in their books, you need to look at your own. Find some writing that you did when you were young, and any other pieces that you've done since then. Which ones were written the most freely? Which ones did you truly *enjoy* writing? Can you see any times when you were trying to copy other authors, and ones where you felt you were truly telling the story *your* way?

You're looking for words that are natural and personal to you. Words that you feel are really appropriate for the sort of story you want to tell, and not just pale copies of someone else's style.

Would you naturally use a controlled, measured pace to your words, with carefully shaped sentences and deliberate over exactly the right description? Or do you use short, punchy, possibly ungrammatical sentences that hit your meaning home?

When you find the right voice for you, you'll feel as if you've come home. You're in the right niche and it fits you perfectly. To do this you may have to accept that, however much you might admire them, you'll never write like authors X or Y or Z. But that's because they're not you.

You should try your hardest to write *authentically*. To write as you, tell the story you want in the words you want to use. Then your writing will have the individuality that will lead people to recognise your voice out of the hundreds of romances published every year.

▶ Tell your characters' story your way.

This is why plotting comes so late in the scheme of this book. In my opinion, it is far more important to spend time with your characters, getting to know them, understand them, building them up, developing them from the inside out, until they are just about functioning on their own.

Then, when you have characters who are so alive that you can almost hear them breathing in the room with you, you will find they will help you tell their story your way.

Creating individual characters

You won't find it easy to create a stunning new plot, but if you work on your characters then they will become individuals in their own right, and this will put an individual twist or flavour into the story you're writing.

Again, don't just try to copy what has gone before. Be yourself. We are all unique, with our own life histories and experiences, and so that is what we bring to writing. If I set a class a basic storyline, with two characters, with names, jobs but little else, and then ask the students to write a beginning to a story where these two people meet, every person will write something different. They will give the characters different ages, different backgrounds, different experiences, and so the stories that started from exactly the same point will take many different paths and end up totally unique and personal.

It's something I know well. I have written over 40 titles now, all of them Modern Romances. There are some themes I have used again and again, but to me each book is different. One Secret Baby plot is Rhys's story (*Their Secret Baby* 2003), another is Morgan's (*His Miracle Baby* 2001), yet another is the story of Pierce and Natalie (*The Unexpected Child* 1997) and none of these heroes are interchangeable, nor are their heroines. They are individual characters whose stories I tell, and as a result the books go along very different lines. That's what gives them their unique and individual quality.

Pace

One of the hardest things to define about a book is whether it has 'pace' or not. Pace is something that you recognise when you are reading, but which you can find very hard to see when you're doing the writing. It isn't just something you can judge by the speed of your fingers flying over the keyboard. Often the parts that are easiest to write turn out to be lacking in pace as they are undisciplined and perhaps self-indulgent. One of the hardest things for a writer is to face the fact that you really should go back and cut out about 50% of your glorious prose! But pace is vital to reader interest and to that Page Turning Quality that you are trying to create.

Most of the topics discussed in Chapter 2 about emotion are relevant to the subject of pace. All those ways of creating emotional punch usually add to the pace of your story too. Dialogue, drama, fast, sharp sentences, emotion – they all add up to PTQ and a pacy read.

But we also have to recap a topic we've looked at already – and that is:

Hooks – again

But this time I'm talking about hooks that you use in your writing, not your plot. Actual writing techniques that will hook your reader and pull her into the story. And hopefully keep her there. And the best place to use these hooks are at the beginning and the end.

The importance of beginnings and endings

Have you ever watched someone in a bookshop when they are browsing, looking for a book to buy? They look along the lines of books until something – the author's name, the cover, the title – catches their eye.

Then they take the book off the shelf. They look at the cover, the 'blurb' on the back and finally, they open it to read the first page.

All in all, this takes seconds. And if that first page doesn't grab them then they will put the book back and you will have lost a chance of a sale.

So obviously the first page is a vital part of your book. What can you do with it to attract a reader?

The first page

The beginning of your story should start with a bang – with an impact that will make the reader want to continue. Ways of doing this are:

▶ **Start with an intriguing opening**
  'Rico Valeron brought the long, powerful car to a smoothly purring halt outside the house and drew on the handbrake. Checking his watch, he turned his key in the ignition, silencing the idling engine. He had plenty of time, he told himself, and settled back in his seat, waiting.' (*The Hostage Bride* 2001)

▶ **Start at a moment of crisis**
  ' "No."
  The single, emphatic syllable was the one word no one was expecting to hear. In the circumstances, it was the last thing that any of the congregation in the tiny village church could have anticipated.' (*The Groom's Revenge* 1997)

▶ **Start with a conversation**
  In fact, one way to really open a story is to start in the middle of a conversation so that the reader wants to know what's going on. My book *The Hired Husband* (1999) starts with the words, 'You want *what?*' from the hero – and the rest of the conversation explains what the heroine has asked him.

▶ **Start with a quiet opening**
  Don't forget that a quiet opening can have impact too, so long as it fits the mood of the book and promises interest to come.

Chapter endings and beginnings

With an opening that draws the reader into your story, you can hope that they will start your book. But then you will want to keep them reading. So you need to put mini hooks at the ends of your chapters that make it impossible to put the book down. A threat, a promise, a realisation, a sudden recollection of a fact that had been forgotten... All these will make your reader want to keep on to find out more.

And if you open the next chapter with another hook – using conversation or suspense or crisis as suggested for the beginning of the book then just a glance at the first page will keep the reader with you.

But if you start a chapter with something like 'Lucy didn't see John for the next three weeks', then the pace will slow, your reader will feel that nothing much is going to happen for a while and so she can safely put your book down and do something else, or sleep.

Sagging middles

It can be wonderfully easy, and exciting, to start out on the first chapter or two of a brand new story, full of confidence and anticipation, with a wonderful plot in your head, and the conviction that *this* is going to be the story that makes you a household name, an instant bestseller.

You introduce your characters, set up the conflict, take them through their first, explosive meeting, add some simmering sexual tensions and then...

And then...

It all slows horribly, like a film projector breaking down, with the film playing in slow motion, slower and slower until it comes to a grinding halt.

You can't take your hero and heroine off to the bedroom, because it wouldn't fit here. You can't have them reconciled because it's way too early. They can't fall into each other's arms because you'd only have half a story.

And you have no idea what will happen next.

You're suffering from that well-known writers' complaint – the sagging middle.

What causes it?

▶ **Characters you don't know well enough**
   If you don't know what your characters are feeling or thinking then you won't be able to tell their story.

▶ **Not enough plot to go round**
   You have set up a conflict that isn't substantial enough to maintain for the length of the book. You might have lots of short-term problems that are easily solved but no major long-term problem – or vice versa.

▶ **Too much back story**
   If the story of what happened to the characters in the past overshadows what's happening now then perhaps *that's* the story you need to tell.

► **You've taken a wrong turning**

You started out with a path clear in your mind but you've headed in the wrong direction somewhere in a scene.

► **You've let too much happen too soon**

You've used up all the tension and excitement, and all the events, without giving the characters time to develop.

► **You've given away too much too early**

You've lost all the mystery, the questions why things happened. There's nothing left to maintain the suspense.

What can you do?
Possible solutions:

► Mentally 'sit down and talk to' your characters. You could try 'interviewing' them and asking them what's going on in their heads.

► Read back through your manuscript to see if you can find where you took that wrong turning.

► Try to rough out a plan for your novel, brainstorming how to develop the plot. You may find you need to go back and *insert* some new scenes that add to the conflict, the motivation or the characters.

Roughly work out what your plot will be, what the conflict is, what events will happen. You can go into as much or as little detail as you like.

Now divide a page up into about 12 sections, one for each chapter. Then divide your plot amongst those 12 chapters, trying to put some significant event, and some emotional development, no matter how small, into each chapter as you go along.

This is only a very basic sort of story plan, just the skeleton on which you're going to hang your novel. And it's not carved in stone. You are not going to be forced to stick to every detail you put into this plan. It's just a rough 'map' to help you keep going forward. But it might help you avoid the sagging middle syndrome next time.

► Try a mind map – start from the basic point of one character perhaps and draw a line as you ask yourself questions – creating branches for each possible different answer. Look at the places where your answers have created more potential 'growth' than you have for the story you have. Would your plot work better if you went that way?

▶ Talk through your plot with someone you trust – let them ask questions. I often find that answering those questions clears the block. Or if it doesn't, then letting them suggest something usually does – I find myself saying 'No, they wouldn't, because...'. And then I find I know just what they *would* do.

▶ You could try going away and doing something practical but boring – the ironing usually works for me. Or just keep ploughing on – sometimes a 'block' is simply 'thinking time' – a point when you need to write slowly, or even pause just to let your imagination catch up. Sleeping on it can often help.

▶ Sometimes you have to accept that this is one of the stories that just isn't going to work. But if you feel it's beyond resuscitation, don't throw it away. Keep the partial draft that you have – you may be able to take scenes from it to put into another story where they might work wonderfully.

Adding subplots

Most series romances are such short books that there is very little room for any subplot. Other characters and stories will take away the focus of the main emotional developments.

But in the slightly longer books, especially those that ask for family oriented stories, you can include other characters' plots. If this is the case, then use the subplot to enhance and illuminate the main plot by letting it mirror that story in some elements and development.

However, always make sure that you read the guidelines and the sort of books that are published in the line you're aiming for to make sure that you are not putting in subplots that shouldn't be there.

12 questions about plotting

1. Does the conflict in this story flow from the characters and their personalities?

2. Is the resolution of the conflict a natural outcome of the plot?

3. Is the romance – the relationship between the two characters – central to the story and not overshadowed by suspense, history, setting, etc?

4. Have I used elements that are tried and tested 'hooks' but tried to put a new twist or element into them?

5. Is there enough conflict to maintain a plot right through to the end?

6. Have my chapter endings and beginnings used hooks to keep the reader interested?

7. Have I started my book with a bang or at least set a tone that will be in the rest of the story?

8. Does my first page hook the reader and pull them in?

9. Does the ending grow from events and my last page leave the reader with the satisfaction that will make her want to buy more?

10. Have I worked out a novel plan so that I have some idea of where I'm going?

11. Have I spaced the action and interest out throughout the book so that there is no 'sagging middle'?

12. Do the subplots, where relevant, mirror or illuminate the main plot and add to the story rather than pad it out?

Exercises

Something to think about

As always, I want you to look at some books.

Beginnings
Try to imagine that you are browsing in a bookshop. Put a selection of books in front of you, then open one at random. Try the 'first page test'.

▶ Read the page – what sort of an opening is it?

▶ Does it hook you, make you want to read on?

▶ *How* does it do that?

▶ If it doesn't hook you – why is that?

▶ How could you rewrite the opening so that it would appeal to you more?

Chapters
Now check the ends of the chapters and look at the beginnings of the new ones.

▶ If you were reading in bed and wondering whether to put the light out, which ones would keep you hooked, unable to put the book down, no matter how late it got?

▶ Why?

▶ Which ones would you find easy to put down – and maybe even have trouble picking up again?

▶ Again, ask yourself why.

Middles

When you're reading a book from beginning to end, study the way that the author keeps the story moving.

See how she gives you bits of information slowly, bit by bit, not all at once.

Notice how there are mixtures of problems, layers to keep the conflict alive. If the plot is one of the 'tried and tested' stories does the author introduce individual details to characters or events that make it not just 'another one of those' stories?

Something to write about

We'll start at the *beginning*.

Write some openings to a story. Try to see if you can start it in several different ways – dialogue – suspense – crisis. See which one works best. Which one would hook you and make you want to read on?

Now do the same with some chapter *endings*. See if you can write some really intriguing endings that would grab at the imagination and make you long to know what was going to happen.

And then try to write the *beginning of the next chapter* so that your imaginary reader just couldn't put it down.

Finally, try to work on a novel plan for the whole of your story. Try working out a chapter by chapter story plan. Then look at the possibilities of a mind map.

Which one of these works best for you? Maybe you should try to use it for the next novel you want to write.

11

The Question 'Why?'

Anyone who knows me, or has been to any of my talks or workshops will know that I always say that the most important question to ask when writing any sort of fiction is *why?*

Why does 'why?' matter so much?

As discussed previously, if you are writing romance, there are only so many plots that you can come up with. It really isn't possible to be stunningly original with any sort of story. But if you give your characters convincing reasons why:

- ▶ they do the things they do
- ▶ they react in the way they do
- ▶ they don't trust each other
- ▶ they fall in love with each other
- ▶ they come around to trusting each other and achieve a resolution

then you have a hope of creating an emotional story with a believable, sustained conflict, pace and a power of page turning quality that will have an editor wanting to read it.

'Why?' helps you create characters

- ▶ Why? makes characters into rounded people with layers and depths to them. It gives them an inner character as well as the one dimension that appears on the page.

- ▶ Why? helps you understand their pasts, their hopes, their fears, their dreams.

- ▶ Why? gives you the reason why the 'Black Moment' is so very black to this particular hero or heroine.

It explains why something that may be possible for one person to shrug off and forget, just can't be done by your character because. . . In other words, it helps to give them that vital vulnerability.

Why? gives you a reason for your heroine going to bed with your hero – or not, if that is what she decides.

It gives you the vitally important before and after for any lovemaking scene.

> She feels vulnerable.
> *Why?*
> Because he has never said a word of love to her.
> He feels betrayed.
> *Why?*
> Because he believes she has only slept with him because... (insert your own reason here).

'Why?' links scenes

Why? gives you the links from one scene to another. And the links from scene to scene are often the hardest things for a writer to grasp. They create a scene – it's wonderfully emotional, passionate sexy, hot. Or it's furiously angry, bitter, full of rage and accusation – and then the characters move on and the point behind that scene may seem to be lost.

But if you know why something happens – and you should know why *everything* happens – then you'll know you'll have to come back to that scene later and link it into what is happening now.

You should never create characters who 'just' do something because that's what you've decided. They should do it 'because' they can't do anything else. And if you give them enough reasons, then even the worst possible behaviour becomes explicable and understandable in the end.

Why? is the thread that holds the wonderful pearl necklace that is your novel together. Why? is the reason everything moves along the path it does and doesn't tie itself up in knots. Why? is the little word that gives logic to your plots, spark to your dialogue and hopefully that little special something that puts the PTQ into your novel and makes it saleable.

'Why?' makes falling in love believable

Never forget that even in a romance, you have to give your hero and heroine reasons why they fall in love with each other. We all know that's what inevitably happens. It's what's expected in a romance. The hero and heroine meet and there is a conflict. The conflict is resolved and there is that happy ever after ending. That's what makes a romance.

But please make it seem at least likely that these two could love each other – and that your ending doesn't just show the sort of behaviour that could end up getting them certified as clinically insane.

Ask them '*why?*'

In a workshop, I was once asked, 'What is the most important part of why the hero and heroine fall in love?' It's a good question. Although it seems so obvious, very often I find that would-be writers haven't thought to ask themselves this – or try to answer it. They know they are writing a romance and they set out to do that. An important – an essential – part of a romance is the happy ending where the couple declare that they are in love with each other and make a commitment to each other for the future. Sometimes, the protagonists have been arguing and fighting – sometimes physically – so much throughout the book that you can't believe they're in the same room together, let alone ready to commit for a lifetime. But they do. And the author expects you to believe they will be happy together.

Although I've been emphasising that to write a good romance you need a conflict that is worth risking everything for, sometimes writing that conflict can get in the way of writing the love story part of the romance. So you need to ask yourself just this question – what is the most important part of why my hero and heroine fall in love? And then you try to answer it – for your characters.

The most important part of why the hero and heroine fall in love – is something intensely personal to them! That is why you must know your characters inside out. You need to create characters that your reader will believe belong together, that there couldn't be anyone else for that character.

This is a fascinating question, because if you look around at the people you know, and the people they're married to – even look at your own partner – and ask 'Why?' 'Why are they together?', 'Why did I marry this man?', you will see that love is not only blind, it's also the exact opposite. It sees things in other people that no one else can find. And these days a woman needs more than just a man who can provide financially for her – a lot of the time, she's more than capable of doing that for herself. So you're looking at emotional fulfilment – two halves of a whole – and for every couple, that's going to be very different.

This is why that question 'why?' will keep coming back and back. You're looking at your characters and thinking 'What does this person most need?' And it may well not be anything like what they *think* they need. That's what makes a developing relationship so intriguing. Obviously sex comes into it in a big way – lust at first sight is far more common than love at first sight. But from then on, to use the image I also used for conflict, it's like peeling an onion – there are layers and layers of the person to discover. And at any point you might discover a discoloured layer, one that puts you off and stops real love forming right there!

We're back to that vital vulnerability in your character – perhaps it's one they don't even know they have. The first chink in their personal emotional armour is the one that lets this person in under their guard so that they can't forget him or her. Then more layers are stripped away, revealing more and more of their vulnerable inner self, until the vital, inner core of the person is exposed. And when the other person touches that, it's like scoring a bullseye. There's no turning back.

So, as I've said, and I'm sure I'll keep saying, you need to know your characters and then you'll know just where that bullseye is and how the other person can reach it and connect with it.

'Why?' can deal with writer's block

Finally, 'why?' can so often help you if you get stuck.

Have you got 'writer's block'? Look at your last scene and say 'Why did this happen?'

Ask your hero – 'Why did you do that?'

Or ask your heroine, 'Why don't you believe him?' (or whatever has been the sticking point in the scene).

And don't take 'I just don't' for an answer.

The answers should help you move on because you'll know how your characters are feeling – and why. If you're really lucky and you're doing it right, it should even open up a whole new line of development, one that will take you right to the heart of their story.

And you'll know why.

Always ask 'Why?' when planning a plot

Some years ago I was in touch with a young and enthusiastic would-be writer. She was a member of this society, had read these books, attended such and such a course and she knew she was going to write for Harlequin Mills & Boon.

She had a wonderful plot, she told me. She wanted to give me a synopsis of her story and would I tell her if I thought it was the sort of thing M&B wanted to buy.

The synopsis told me that her heroine inherited an island from a distant relative; when she got there the hero was already living on the island. He was furious with the heroine and hated her on sight. . .

Here I interrupted – 'Hang on – why?'

'Why what?'

'Why did he hate her on sight?'

'He just did.'

'But why?'

'Well that's what heroes do.'

'But why?'

Some minutes later, when she realised I wasn't going to give in, she grudgingly tossed out, 'Well, he thought he should have inherited the island himself.'

The rest of her synopsis involved the 'hero' kidnapping the heroine and holding her prisoner on the island ('Because he wanted to'). He called her every name under the sun, laughed at her and told her she was shallow and stupid, took all her nice clothes and threw them into the sea (what was that question again? Why?) He also threw her CD player and all her CDs into the sea, had sex with her (she 'fought against it but very soon gave in'. Er – why?) then finally she saw a little sense and ran away. But she couldn't stay away from him and she went back to the island to see him (all together now – why?) He said he was sorry and he had fallen in love with her from the start and would she marry him – and she said yes. Why?

This is an extreme example. An example of a plot that was based on the mistaken belief that romance heroes 'always' treat their women very badly – for no good reason – and in spite of this the women fall madly in love with their tormentors and marry them. The hero is abusive, hateful, probably has criminal tendencies, just about rapes the heroine – and then says he loves her and she settles down to marriage with him – the woman must be insane!

This one is a bit far-fetched but if you add in some major justifications, you might just get the beginnings of a plot out of it. Perhaps the hero had originally been left the island in his grandfather's will but just before his death grandpa had married a much younger second wife who had survived him. She had then bequeathed the island to the heroine. The hero had desperately wanted the island because it was where his mother and father were buried and he had been led to believe that the heroine intended to turn the place into a tourist village, without a care of anyone else's feelings. You'd still have to work pretty hard to make some of this supposed hero's actions understandable, never mind justified, but at least you'd have a start.

To try to illustrate this point, I've included here a synopsis of one of my books. This serves two purposes.

▶ It gives an example of a synopsis. Many romance publishers ask for either a query letter and a synopsis or a synopsis and three chapters (a partial) so you will need to have some idea how to write one. This is a long synopsis. Some publishers like Mills & Boon only ask for short one. (There are more details on synopses in Chapter 14.)

▶ There are two versions of the synopsis. The first one just gives the details of the events in the book without answering that important question 'Why?'. The second version has the reasons why things happen added and in bold type so that you can see the difference. These insertions explain both characters' behaviour much more clearly, deepen the motivation, and make the story more believable.

Example synopsis 1

Constantine's Revenge by Kate Walker

Grace Vernon and Greek tycoon Constantine Kiriazis were to have been married, but the weekend before the wedding her stepsister Paula accused him of seducing her. She claimed that he had been coming on to her ever since they had first met, refusing to take no for an answer. He put pressure on more and more until in the end she had found herself succumbing and had slept with him. But now she feels so guilty that she just has to tell her sister the truth.

Grace initially totally rejects the whole story, but slowly Constantine's own behaviour seems to indicate that something is up. Instead of immediately reassuring her that nothing happened and that Paula's story is just a pack of lies, he becomes coldly distant and refuses to even answer her questions.

She decides that the only thing she can do is to call off the wedding. When she finally persuades Paula to tell her the truth – that the supposed seduction never happened – Grace is overjoyed and believes that the wedding can now take place. But Constantine has been deeply hurt by her doubting him. He cannot marry someone who does not trust him as absolutely as he believes his future wife should. He calls off the engagement and tells her he never wants to see her ever again.

Two years later, Grace's gay friend, Ivan is holding a Turn Back the Clock party to celebrate his 30th birthday, and to Grace's horror she finds that he has invited Constantine. But after some initial hostility, they find that they cannot deny the spark that originally brought them together and which is still there between them.

At the end of the evening, Constantine takes Grace home and when he kisses her the passion that has been simmering between them all evening flares up out of control. That night they become lovers for the first time. She dreams of the delayed wedding now taking place as the final proof of their reconciliation.

But the following day Constantine cruelly disillusions her. He has no intention of marrying her. Their love-making was purely physical passion, nothing more. But he admits that he is addicted to *that*, and would be more than willing to keep her as his mistress until he grows tired of her. He could never marry someone who doesn't trust him completely, but that fact will make her the perfect mistress because she will always be that little bit on edge and unsure of him and so will go to great lengths to make sure he is happy in order to keep him by her side.

In return, he will keep her in the manner to which he believes she would like to become accustomed. She will find he is a very generous lover, and he will not make too many demands on her (except physically).

Grace accepts the relationship he offers even though it is very much second best. And Constantine proves himself to be as generous as he promised, in every way but emotionally.

After some months her hopes grow when Constantine suggests they go on holiday together in Greece and takes her back to his family home where they once shared a wonderful week just after he had proposed to her when he introduced her to his family.

But her hopes are cruelly dashed when Constantine's mother and father, who had been away visiting his married sister, return home unexpectedly early and instead of being introduced to them again she finds that she is hurried out of the house and taken back to England. Her hurt is made all the worse when Constantine declares that his parents have never been introduced to any of his mistresses. That is an honour he reserves solely for the woman he will make his wife.

Grace tries to break off their relationship once and for all. But Constantine will not let her go. Grace says she cannot live like this any more and she needs some time on her own.

Some days later Grace is at a party organised by her bosses at the advertising agency where she works. Constantine is not with her. One of the company's clients who has made it plain that he fancies her becomes rather drunk and pesters her all evening. When she leaves he follows her and tries to kiss her, declaring that he wants her, that he has heard rumours that she and Constantine have split up and that if she's looking for a rich man to replace her former lover then he'll be only too happy to oblige. When she tries to push him away he becomes more insistent until she runs from him in fear.

Shocked and distressed, Grace heads straight for Constantine. Constantine admits that he loves her. He begs her to forgive him and asks her to be his wife, and of course she accepts his proposal.

Example synopsis 2

Constantine's Revenge by Kate Walker

Grace Vernon and Greek tycoon Constantine Kiriazis were to have been married, but the weekend before the wedding her stepsister Paula accused him of seducing her. She claimed that he had been coming on to her ever since they had first met, refusing to take no for an answer. He put pressure on more and more until in the end she had found herself succumbing and had slept with him. But now she feels so guilty that she just has to tell her sister the truth.

Grace initially totally rejects the whole story, but slowly Constantine's own behaviour seems to indicate that something is up. Instead of immediately reassuring her that nothing happened and that Paula's story is just a pack of lies, he becomes coldly distant and refuses to even answer her questions. **He believes that she should not even need to ask, that she should trust him completely, and his pride holds him back from even trying to explain.**

Once the seed of doubt is planted in her mind, Grace is forced to wonder if perhaps she might have been partially responsible for Constantine's actions. She has always held back from consummating their relationship physically, wanting their wedding night to be their first night as lovers. But it has been increasingly

clear that Constantine has found the waiting harder and harder to cope with. Knowing that he has had other lovers before her, she is afraid that his frustrated passion might have driven him to seduce Paula. She is very protective of her younger stepsister and is completely unaware of the fact that Paula is deeply jealous of her.

When her father advises her that if she has any doubts at all, it is better to err on the side of caution, she decides that the only thing she can do is to call off the wedding, believing in her heart that it will only be a postponement, not a cancellation. When she finally persuades Paula to tell her the truth – that the supposed seduction never happened – Grace is overjoyed and believes that the wedding can now take place. But Constantine has been deeply hurt by her doubting him. He cannot marry someone who does not trust him as absolutely as he believes his future wife should. He calls off the engagement and tells her he never wants to see her ever again.

Two years later, Grace's gay friend, Ivan is holding a Turn Back the Clock party to celebrate his 30th birthday, and to Grace's horror she finds that he has invited Constantine in a deliberate attempt to see the two reconciled. But after some initial hostility, they find that they cannot deny the spark that originally brought them together and which is still there between them. Grace manages to persuade Constantine to agree to abide by the theme of the party, and they agree to 'turn back the clock' and act as if Paula's lies and the cancelled wedding had never happened, at least for one night.

At the end of the evening, Constantine takes Grace home and when he kisses her the passion that has been simmering between them all evening flares up out of control. That night they become lovers for the first time. Grace believes that Constantine has forgiven her for her past doubts and that by making love with him and not insisting on waiting for her wedding night, she has proved that she does trust him. She dreams of the delayed wedding now taking place as the final proof of their reconciliation.

But the following day Constantine cruelly disillusions her. He has no intention of marrying her. Their love-making was purely physical passion, nothing more. But he admits that he is addicted to *that*, and would be more than willing to keep her as his mistress until he grows tired of her. He could never marry someone who doesn't trust him completely, but that fact will make her the perfect mistress because she will always be that little bit on edge and unsure of him and so will go to great lengths to make sure he is happy in order to keep him by her side.

In return, he will keep her in the manner to which he believes she would like to become accustomed. She will find he is a very generous lover, and he will not make too many demands on her (except physically).

Grace knows that she still loves Constantine desperately and that it would destroy her if he was to walk away from her again. So she accepts the relationship he offers even though it is very much second best. And Constantine proves himself to be as generous as he promised, in every way but emotionally. But Grace hangs on to the hope that as long as he is with her she still has a chance of winning his heart once again.

After some months her hopes grow when Constantine suggests they go on holiday together in Greece and takes her back to his family home where they once shared a wonderful week just after he had proposed to her when he introduced her to his family. **Finding herself alone with him in this way, she allows herself to wonder if perhaps he plans to repeat their private history and propose all over again.**

But her hopes are cruelly dashed when Constantine's mother and father, who had been away visiting his married sister, return home unexpectedly early and instead of being introduced to them again she finds that she is hurried out of the house and taken back to England. Her hurt is made all the worse when Constantine declares that his parents have never been introduced to any of his mistresses. That is an honour he reserves solely for the woman he will make his wife.

Shattered and believing she will never have his love again, Grace tries to break off their relationship once and for all. But Constantine will not let her go. **He cannot live without her, he says. When challenged that that sounds remarkably like love, he responds that even if it is love, he has no intention of acting on it. Grace's lack of trust in the past will always come between them.** Grace says she cannot live like this any more and she needs some time on her own.

Some days later Grace is at a party organised by her bosses at the advertising agency where she works. Constantine is not with her. One of the company's clients who has made it plain that he fancies her becomes rather drunk and pesters her all evening. When she leaves he follows her and tries to kiss her, declaring that he wants her, that he has heard rumours that she and Constantine have split up and that if she's looking for a rich man to replace her former lover then he'll be only too happy to oblige. When she tries to push him away he becomes more insistent until she runs from him in fear.

Shocked and distressed, Grace acts purely on instinct, and heads straight for Constantine. **She doesn't care if he loves her or not. She needs him. It is his arms she wants round her, his strength she wants to lean against. When Constantine points out that Ivan, with whom she has been friends for over ten years lives much closer and would have been a safe haven for her, she can only say that the thought of turning to Ivan or anyone else never even crossed her mind. Faced with this evidence of her complete, instinctive trust of him, Constantine admits that he has never stopped loving her, that he has never really been able to let her go, and that is why he wanted to keep her with him any way he could. He had already realised that he was acting out of hurt pride, that in his own way he has been as distrusting as he accused her of being, and that he'd decided that he was going to ask her to marry him again because he couldn't face a future which didn't have her in it.**

The real reason he hurried her away from his parents' home was because he knew his mother would take one look at her son with Grace and know that he was still crazy about her – and she wouldn't have been able to keep quiet about it. He begs her to forgive him and asks her to be his wife, and of course, **believing in his love and knowing she has never stopped loving him** she accepts his proposal.

12 questions about the question 'Why?'

1. Do I know why my hero and heroine are who they are?

2. Do I know why they are where they are?

3. Do I know why they react to each other in the way that they do at first meeting?

4. Do I know why these reactions change at stages through the book?

5. Do I know why my hero falls in love with the heroine and vice versa? And why they declare/don't reveal that love?

6. Do I know why my heroine says no to the hero when she does?

7. Do I know why they make love at the point they do? And why they react as they do afterwards?

8. If I hit writer's block is it because I don't know why my hero or heroine is doing what they're doing/has done what they did?

9. Have I made my hero or heroine do something because it fits the plot I am trying to write, rather than knowing why they would do this?

10. Do I know why arguments/alienation happen dividing my hero and heroine from each other?

11. Do I know why the Black Moment feels so bad to both of them?

12. Do I know why they can both come to a reconciliation and create a happy ending that is right for them?

Exercises

Something to think about
Again, this has a couple of different parts.

Reading
The first one, as so often, has to do with looking at your reading. This is vitally important, because as you are reading you should be observing and learning as well as absorbing the story. You read as a writer in order to learn how other

writers do the things that we've been discussing.

So, as you're reading, watch and see how the author you're reading answers the question 'why?' in their story.

▶ Maybe they'll make the character say it outright.

▶ Or maybe it will be conveyed through their thoughts when you're in their point of view.

▶ Or maybe it will come out through a contradictory description – he says something but his tone, his expression, a gesture, indicates that he means the exact opposite.

▶ Or perhaps someone else in the room reacts in a way that makes it clear that what has been said is just not the case.

Watch this happening and see how so often you would barely notice it as you were reading – but you'd absorb it just the same.

Thinking

Secondly – and this is partly the 'writing about' bit as well – remember when you were a child – or if that's too long ago and you have children yourself, think about them. Think about that infuriating way they have of sometimes just asking 'Why? Why? Why?' until you feel you're going insane.

> 'Joey, pick up your toys.'
> 'Why?'
> 'Because if you don't they'll get broken.'
> 'Why?'
> 'Because someone might tread on them.'
> 'Why?
> 'Because they won't see them there.'
> 'Why?'
> 'Because...'
> 'Why?'

Eventually there will come a point when one of two things will happen:

▶ either you will lose all patience and just say 'Because I say so!'

▶ or you will give a long and detailed explanation of exactly what will happen if Joey leaves his toys on the floor, which is much more information than he ever wanted.

Something to write about

Try asking your characters 'Why?'. Take a point where, for example, your hero has behaved appallingly to his heroine – or vice versa. Get them in the same room together – and start asking questions.

'Why did you do that?'
'I felt angry/hurt/betrayed.'
'Why?'
'Because I thought that you meant. . .'
'Why would you think that?'

Write down the dialogue. Then go back and look at it, remembering the things you've learned from your reading. Put in the thoughts, the viewpoint, the actions etc that reveal the truth of betray the reality of what they are thinking and feeling – and the real answer why – the one that starts to reveal that inner core of vulnerability that you (and your hero/heroine) are trying to aim for.

12

The Intense Black Moment

Why is the ending or, in fact, the point just before the ending – that point where everything seems lost and your hero and heroine and your reader are in despair – so important?

Looking at emotion again

Let's look again at what your reader wants from a romance when she picks it up. Within varying degrees, according to the line you're writing for, your reader is looking for – that word again – an *emotional* read. She knows in advance what the ending is going to be – everyone knows that. This is a romance we're writing. It's going to have that happy ever after ending, with either a wedding or the promise of one on the last page.

So there will be no surprises there. Not for the reader, and not for you as a writer. You're going to end this story in the tried and tested way that romances have ended for years. Everyone knows that, unlike Rhett Butler at the end of *Gone With the Wind*, your hero isn't going to turn around and say 'Frankly my dear, I don't give a damn!' and walk out of your heroine's life.

But first you have to get him there.

Keeping the reader in suspense

Because there's no surprise about the ending, you need to put in some pretty hard work in the sections before it. You need to make the reader worry. You need to make her doubt. She knows there's that happy ever after coming, but just for a little while, you need to have her on tenterhooks, you need to have her feeling that perhaps this time it might not work out. She needs to have the thought, 'And just *how* are they going to get out of this one?' cross her mind. And she needs to wonder, just for a moment, whether they will.

If the ending comes too easily, if your heroine and hero simply have to say something straightforward – 'Oh I never meant that! What I meant was...' or 'That wasn't any "other woman" – that was my cousin!', 'But I love you!', or whatever, then the ending is going to fall rather flat and be unmemorable.

If you have spent so much time building up the intensity of the emotion and the conflict and you've created a pacy, page turning quality novel with lots of passion in it – then the worst moment should be something really deep, really bad, something very painful for both your characters. Something that can't just be mended with a quick explanation. After the emotional roller-coaster ride that I hope you've put your reader through she's going to find a 'cop-out' ending very disappointing and unsatisfactory. The more emotional the ending, the more conflict and misunderstanding there is to be resolved, the more passionate your hero and heroine are about each other and their own goals, then the more your reader is going to enjoy that happy ever after ending when she gets to it.

But if you don't give her the conflict that comes before – if the Black Moment isn't black but only shades of grey, then she will skim through it, put the book down – and possibly even hurry on to the next one to get back to the emotional stuff. If she does that then your book will be quickly forgotten.

What you want is the sort of response to your ending where the reader finishes the story, possibly even with a tear in her eye, and wants to sit still for a quiet moment just to think and reflect on how much she enjoyed the book. You want her to think back over certain scenes, to relive them once more.

Writing a double climax

I have always liked to write a 'double ending' or 'double climax'. This means that you bring your heroine and hero to a point where it looks at last as if things are going right. You can clear some parts of the conflict out of the way – this is why you need a multi-layered conflict so that there are some parts you can resolve while still leaving something that isn't sorted out.

Now it looks as if they are getting closer and things have been sorted out and peace is gradually forming. You make it look as if that happy ending is on the horizon – and then just as they are about to fall into each other's arms, you throw another spanner in the works and tear them apart again.

This doesn't mean that you introduce something new. It's best if you bring back in something that was mentioned at the beginning of the book, or close to it. Something that seems to have been glossed over but still needs sorting out – and that can still come between them and their happy ever after. Here's an example.

His Miracle Baby
The hero and heroine separated because he was adamant he didn't want children. But she found she was pregnant and now she has his baby.

The first conflict is that he has to find out that the baby is his – then when that is cleared up, he has to tell her why he didn't want children (another crisis) then they find a sort of a peace.

Now he wants the little girl but the heroine is still not sure that he wants her and not just the child. Or that he wants her for herself and not just because she comes along with the child. As a result, there is a second Black Moment to be resolved.

The destruction of all their hopes
You'll remember that in Chapter 3, I said that you needed to make your conflict something that was worth fighting over – something that was worth losing

everything, including the love of your life, for. And this is what should come home at the Black Moment of the book.

It should seem possible that your hero and heroine can lose everything they really value. That their lives will never be the same. That their happiness has been ruined – apparently for ever. They might have won whatever battle they thought they were fighting, but by doing so they've lost the war – the emotional fight for each other's love.

If you do that, then the happy ever after ending will be all the sweeter for your reader and you'll really get that 'Aaah!' moment as she closes the book.

What is the best point for the Black Moment?

Another question I've been asked in workshops is: 'Where in the book should the Black Moment come? In the very last chapter? In the last but one?'

I'm tempted to give the answer that it should come *at the right place*. But I realise that this isn't terribly helpful.

You see, if you know your characters and your plot then there will be a perfect moment for that Black Moment – that worst possible point in your characters' relationships and then it will almost write itself. Again, as with all the so-called 'rules' – there aren't any! There isn't a precise page or line reference at which the lowest point between your protagonists should hit home.

But the important thing to remember is that you don't want to waste that low point – the Black Moment. You don't want to bring it in too early so that the last section of the book is a let down, feeling second rate compared to the growing tension before. Because as I've said, that's what you're aiming for – the build up and gathering speed of tension that leads to the Black Moment becoming totally inevitable, unavoidable, so that the reader can see it looming on the horizon, darkening the atmosphere for a time before it comes.

Also, if you have that moment come in too early, then you are left with a messy 'tidying up' section – and you have to have some very good reasons why your hero and heroine don't just part for good – or, equally, don't just sit down and talk things out and get everything clear.

So I try to make that moment as late as possible in the book – as late as possible while still leaving time and the possibility of sorting everything out in the end. Remember that the Black Moment is one of two 'emotional climaxes' that the reader is looking for. That and the moment when the couple declare their love for each other are what stay in a reader's mind. So don't waste it.

The whole idea is to keep the tension getting tighter and tighter with the Black Moment occurring as close to the end as possible so that it really appears that 'all is lost'. Then your resolution will be that much sweeter when it occurs. Of course there are other mini-Black Moments earlier when things seem to be coming right and then, for one reason or another, they don't.

But this isn't something that can be plotted out ahead of time. It grows organically from who the people are and what matters to them and what circumstances they find themselves in.

The story structure has the book opening with a major hook, with either the hero or the heroine (or both) at a moment of crisis and then going through a series of two steps forward, one step back (a sort of ebb and flow) on the way to another major Black Moment very close to the end. The final part of the story resolves both the external and the internal conflicts.

12 questions about the intense Black Moment

1. Is this really the lowest point I can bring my characters to – the point where it appears there will be no happy ending? Or can I go still lower?

2. Why is this particular problem worse than any other that has gone before?

3. Does the Black Moment follow naturally from the events of the plot and the core characters and beliefs of my hero and heroine?

4. Is the Black Moment an emotional one rather than a physical danger or a solution to a mystery?

5. If others have a hand in it – is it the effect that their actions and/or announcement have on my characters that make it truly black?

6. Is it a real problem and not just something that could be resolved by a question or two?

7. Can the reader as well as the characters not see how it can be resolved?

8. Are there elements in this scene that I should keep back, even from the reader, so that it is as shocking as it can be?

9. Does it have in it the seeds of the happy 'climax' – that happy ending that will follow it?

10. Have I placed the Black Moment at the best possible place in the story where it has most impact? Do I still have room to resolve the fall out from it?

11. Have I made sure that I have seeming proof of any accusations that are made so that the person believing them is justified and not just stupid?

12. Have I some further proof that I can bring in later as evidence that this is wrong – and not just that the hero or heroine says 'Oh well – I believe you. . .'?

Exercises

Something to think about

As you know by now – I'm going to ask you to look at the books you've been reading – and especially at the endings.

See which ones had endings you've really enjoyed – the ones that have made your heart beat just that little bit faster or that have made you bite your lip in concern. The ones that have made you think 'This can never get healed/mended/explained/resolved' and had you really worrying for the hero and heroine.

▶ Look at the last couple of chapters and see if there is a 'double climax'.

▶ Does everything seem to be going right and then something else comes in to spoil things?

▶ Does this 'other thing' follow naturally from clues laid down at the beginning of the book or does it feel awkward and imposed from the outside?

▶ Is some of the conflict sorted out earlier so that the Black Moment comes as something devastating?

Then think about your own story's conflict.

▶ Is the ending too abrupt?

▶ Or maybe it has too little to resolve?

▶ Does it come to a real low point just before the resolution, so that things seem terrible – and the ending seems wonderful in contrast?

▶ Or does it just fade out with a whimper and not a bang – with an ending where all they have to do is just explain a couple of points and it's all over?

▶ Have you really made it look as if your hero and heroine have reached the end and that they now have no further chance of saving their relationship? Or is there is no hope of a future together?

▶ Do you feel that if someone just shook them and said, 'Come on, you two – start talking' – they could patch it up in a second?

Something to write about

Looking at your own points of *conflict* that you've worked on throughout this, write your own ending – dealing with one aspect of the problem first and clearing that up, but then, as things calm down, bringing in the second, most difficult situation.

This should arise naturally from the plot – i.e. you should have laid down clues to it earlier – something that the heroine is keeping from the hero for example – so that inevitably it will come out just at the worst possible moment and even though they've been working towards forgiveness and reconciliation, this blows up right in their faces.

Using dialogue as much as possible, try to create a mini-crisis – an apparent resolution to that mini-crisis and then write a real Black Moment for your characters.

But remember that you will always need to get them out of it! So don't put them into a situation that you have no idea how to solve.

13

A Believable Happy Ending

We've now arrived at the very last of the 12 points. I think we've come a long way since we started out together on the first point about emotion. I hope you've come a long way with your own work and have made a lot of progress towards getting it the way you – and hopefully an editor – would want it.

So – that ending. Why is it so important? Well, for one very obvious reason – you have to end your book so you want to do it well. But there's another vital point to remember.

Achieving reader satisfaction

▶ Your first page and the way it (hopefully) hooks a reader in is the thing that sells *this* book that you are writing now.

▶ The ending, and the way your book closes will be important in selling the *next* one.

You want to leave your reader with that 'Aaah!' moment – that feeling of delight and satisfaction so that when she closes the book, she does so reluctantly and wants to linger in the warmth that she feels as she reads the last pages.

You want her to regret that the book is finished but be glad that it ended the way it did. And you want her to spend a little while thinking about what she has read and remembering how much she enjoyed it.

Now we all know that there is never any real surprise in the happy ending to a romance. No one ever says, 'Well, that's amazing! They ended declaring their love for each other and living happily ever after! I never expected that!'

Obviously you know that it isn't possible to write a completely unexpected ending to your romance, but you do you need to give your reader a totally *satisfactory* ending.

Winding it all up

The ending is easy. Isn't it? Or it should be. You wind everything up, deal with all the knots and problems, resolve the conflict, throw your hero and heroine into each others' arms, have a wonderfully emotional reconciliation – and they live happily ever after.

Done. Simple. The book is finished.

Well – not always. It's dealing with all the knots and the problems that can cause the writer difficulties. And that's why I have used those important words – a *believable* and a *satisfactory* happy ending.

What is not a satisfactory ending?

We're back to that word – emotion – again. If you have created an emotional story that has grabbed your reader and got her totally involved with your characters, then you don't want to sell her short in the ending. Here are some of the things that she doesn't want:

▶ Not a simple, easy, 'Sorry love, but I was in a bad mood' sort of ending.

▶ No instant falling into each other's arms and forgetting the pain and the conflict in the blink of an eyelid.

▶ No ending that is resolved by some magical trick – the appearance of a will that solves all the financial troubles – the 'other woman' suddenly getting an attack of the guilts – the amazing cure of the terrible deadly disease.

You're a writer, not a magician waving a magic wand to solve everything. You created these characters and put them in this situation. (If you did it right then *they* put themselves into it.) Now you and they have to get out of it.

But first they need to go through a learning and thinking time.

The dark night of the soul – or the switch
In order to reach the happy ending from the lowest point of the Black Moment, obviously something has to change. Your characters have to realise that:

▶ they desperately want to do something to change the situation; and

▶ there is something they can do about it, even if it's only to beg; or

▶ something beyond their control – or some new information – forces a change on them.

Daphne Clair and Robyn Donald call the period between the Black Moment and the happy ending the 'dark night of the soul'. The dark night can last only a moment or it can keep the lovers apart for a year or so (though it shouldn't take up a large amount of space in the actual book – this is not a point at which you want the reader to lose sight of the characters she has become so involved with).

This is going to make them fully understand just what has happened, why it has happened and what they can do about it. It is usually a time of great pain, a terrible sense of loss, but it is also a time when they learn a lot about themselves, about their lover, and about anything that has happened between them. At some point they will make the switch from being lost and forlorn to the moment when they can find some way out of the darkness. They will come out fighting and set out to tackle the problem that has come between them and the person they love. And that will lead to the happy ending.

Your characters stay in character

For one thing, your characters are going to retain the character you gave them. So if the hero has been arrogant and domineering all the way through, he's going to keep some of that pride even when he crumbles and admits his love.

If the heroine has been provoking him all the way through, then she's going to continue to provoke and drive him crazy at the end too – though she'll probably do it in a softer and gentler way, a more loving way.

And if there are other people involved – say, people whose lies or interference have helped to create the conflict, then their part needs to be resolved, and the hero and heroine's reactions to them need to be sorted out.

You don't want the reader thinking – yes, but what about so-and-so? Or – but what would happen if they came up against *that* again. If your reader thinks that maybe at some time in the future, the person who caused all the trouble, or the situation that created the conflict might come back again and cause problems, then they aren't going to *believe* in the happy ever after ending. And an unbelievable ending is an unsatisfactory one.

Happy ever after

You need to make sure that when your reader looks at your hero and heroine in each other's arms on the last page of your book, she is convinced they have a good chance of still feeling this way in the years to come and still being together so that they can celebrate their golden wedding anniversary. To do that, you have to make sure that just as the conflict that pushed them apart came from inside them, from the deepest core of their personalities, so the resolution of that conflict, the answers to the problems, the forgiveness and understanding that is needed to move on, also comes right from their hearts.

Obviously, you have to clear up all the awkward points and problems, the misunderstandings, the lies someone else might have told, the secrets they have kept. But the really important change has to come from within them.

A union of equals

You also must make sure that the ending has a form of balance.

An unequal ending is one where either the hero or the heroine does all the giving. They do all the apologising for what is often a joint problem; a situation that both of them have created. Or they give up what seems like everything and the other doesn't give at all.

So, for example, if part of the conflict was because the heroine wanted a job that the hero really thought was too dangerous, an equal ending is not her deciding to give up the job so that he can feel better. Or, necessarily, for him to give way totally and understand. There should be a compromise. They should meet each other halfway. One of the ways this could be solved is for him to say he understands her need to do this job and he'll support her. But if, by this time, she has realised how she would feel if someone she loved as desperately as she loves him was killed doing something that was dangerous, she might already have said no to the idea.

A modern relationship – and a romance is really a 'relationship novel' – usually works on some form of compromise that both partners can live with. So your characters need to work out the sort of balance they can live with – there should be no winners, no losers, just a union of equals.

Don't rush the ending

Finally, don't rush your endings. Yes, it's the closing of the book, the tying up of all the ends, but that doesn't mean the reader doesn't want to enjoy it. She wants to live through this as much as she wanted to live through all the rest of their story.

▶ Take your time.

▶ Make it as emotional as you can.

▶ Make it fit your hero and heroine and the characters you've given them.

▶ Above all, make it fit the story you've been telling. Keep the mood the same in your last chapter as it has been through the rest of the story.

If you've written a sizzlingly sexy story then give it an equally sizzling ending. If your book has been light-hearted and fun then put laughter into its conclusion.

'But you said...'

But don't just turn your ending into a stream of discussion, with nothing but explanations and 'But you said. . .' and 'But I didn't mean it. . .' type of dialogue.
The ways to avoid doing this include:

▶ Remembering the points about using 'business' in the chapter on dialogue and use them here too.

▶ Making sure that your hero and heroine stay real and alive and in character in this last section.

▶ Giving them things to do.

▶ Moving them from place to place even if it's only from room to room, or within the one room where they are.

▶ Realising your ending and explanation scene doesn't have to run smoothly straight through. You can introduce some sort of diversion – the brief arrival of someone else, or a phone call, or an event outside. This can break up the scene, change the mood of the moment, move your characters on to some point that perhaps they had forgotten.

▶ Remembering that explanations don't have to be static – and nor do your characters.

Proving the case

When there has been some situation that needs actual proof to clear it up, make sure that you can provide it – not necessarily for the characters, but for the reader's satisfaction.

For example, if the heroine needs to prove that she didn't marry the hero for his money, make her throw his money back in his face, or show she's used it to found a charitable organisation. Of course, by the time you get to the ending, the hero, having been through his own 'dark night', will have come to the conclusion that he just doesn't need this proof. But she will want to give him the evidence to prove her love as well. This is another example of the sort of equal ending that you need.

But please, if your heroine has spent the whole book doing something like accusing the hero of having another woman, and although he has protested his innocence she has never believed him, don't make her just have a sudden change of heart now and say, 'Yes, I believe you.' This will make her look stupid for never having believed him before. If the situation is so bad that proof is needed, give proof. But also remember that the proof of someone's love is that they don't need that evidence to convince them.

We come back to the point about choosing the reasons for your conflict carefully, because you will always have to clear them up in the final chapter. You will need to get the balance right so that your reader believes that your hero and heroine can trust each other, that they do trust each other, and that any difficulties that have been between them have been cleared up in both a factual and an emotional way.

Commitment – for now – or forever?

I've already mentioned that the traditional and usual ending to a romance story is the conventional wedding. Or, if the hero and heroine are husband and wife who were previously married and have been driven apart by past events and are now separated, then they will renew their wedding vows either publicly or privately.

This is not a moral judgement and ending but a form of shorthand that is accepted by most readers as an indication of a wholehearted and long-term commitment to each other that the couple want to mark in a formal way.

This is the 'tried and tested' ending to a romance. But with the arrival of new 'chick-lit' style romances and the Red Dress Ink imprint, there is more scope for a less obvious ending to your book.

It is possible, particularly in the chick-lit stories where Mr Right is perhaps more accurately described as Mr Right Now, not to have the formal, legal commitment of the marriage and wedding vows. But the reader still wants to feel that the couple are right together, that they care deeply enough to make some sort of a commitment to each other, whether to live together or be in an exclusive relationship, for example.

The important thing about the ending to a romance is that positive and hopeful feeling that these two have won through to a deep and meaningful relationship that will endure. That is what the reader is looking for at the end – it is why she bought a romance in the first place – and that is what the author should give her.

Finding just the right ending

Endings can be breathlessly exciting resolutions, where happiness is snatched from despair at the very last minute. They can be deeply gentle and tender, or powerfully sexy and fiercely passionate, or even humorous. But they should leave your reader on a high where all her dreams and hopes for this couple have been satisfied.

It can take several attempts to create just the right ending for the particular story that you are writing, but it's worth the effort, because it is what lives in your reader's mind, after she's closed the covers on this book, and that makes her look for your name on other books in the future.

Epilogues

Personally, I prefer not to use an Epilogue unless I really have to. Adding anything – even a description of the wedding day – takes away the impact of the happy ending. It brings the reader down slightly, slackens the pace and dilutes the emotional effect you've been aiming for.

But sometimes there is no alternative but to add something at the end of the story. For example, if you have some problems (other than the emotional and loving relationship between the hero and heroine) that need to be sorted out, then these sometimes need to be dealt with in an epilogue or extra pages in the last chapter.

I once needed to do this when my story involved a heroine whose first baby had died. Although the relationship between her and her hero had been sorted out, for full emotional closure, the reader needed to see that in the future she would have children who lived and thrived. So I added an extra section to that effect, showing her with her husband and son and a new baby on the way.

It's not just the love story that needs to be wrapped up in the ending. You need to clear up any worry the reader or your characters might have. The reader wants to know that the characters you have created have a hope of fulfilling the fantasy of 'and they lived happily ever after'.

If the reader has enjoyed the rest of the book, but found the ending unsatisfactory, then that will be what she will remember when she sees your name on a book in the future. But if you have given her the complete romance reading experience, with an ending that lingers in her memory, then she will be reaching for your next book as soon as she sees it.

12 questions about the happy ending

1. Does my ending result naturally from the characters of the hero and heroine – not the magical intervention of fate, etc?

2. Does it resolve all the problems and questions of the story, leaving no point where the reader will say, 'But. . .'?

3. Does the ending seem like the beginning of a life together for the characters that the reader will believe will last?

4. Is the last chapter just a list of 'but you said. . .' dialogue? Have I varied the tone of the dialogue?

5. Do my characters have 'business' things to do while sorting out their conflicts/ problems, etc?

6. If there is anyone else involved in the 'sorting out' process have I dealt with them?

7. Have I ended my book on an uplifting, positive note – a commitment to each other or a marriage, if wanted?

8. Is the ending appropriate to the line I am writing?

9. Are the problems resolved in character for my hero and heroine?

10. Is the ending happy enough? For instance, if there are any problems other than in the love story – a cot death or miscarriage for example – have I shown that they are resolved?

11. Is the ending one of equals – each giving and forgiving where necessary – not just one giving and one taking?

12. Even though the reader knew this was what was coming all the time have I managed to find one small way to surprise her?

Exercises

Something to think about

You should have a pretty good idea what I going to say by now. Look at your reading, at the books you've recently enjoyed, and in particular look at their endings.

But now you have a new way to look at them – not just as an enjoyable part of the story but also as the 'winding up' section at the end of all that emotion and conflict.

▶ How does the author you've read handle that job?

▶ Does she answer all the questions you wanted answering? Does she leave you with any 'Buts...'? (I'm not including deliberate 'Buts...' here – the sort where an author leaves something unanswered because she plans to bring it into another book, when this is one of a series.)

▶ Do you feel satisfied and that the ending was an enjoyable part of the story?

▶ Or did you feel it was just tacked on to bring it to a close? Did you feel that it fitted the sort of story the whole book was about?

Now think about your own story.

▶ What sort of a **plot** is it?

▶ What sort of **emotion** and **conflict** have you created?

▶ What is the overall **tone** and **atmosphere** of the story?

▶ What sort of **characters** have you created – how can you keep them in character?

▶ So what sort of an **ending** do you think *you* will need to make it a satisfactory and a satisfying one?

Something to write about

Having looked at the atmosphere and tone of your story, and decided what's needed for the ending as well – what you need to do now is to make a list.

List every little thing that needs to be sorted out in the ending. Remember the point about the 'double climax' – the two stage Black Moment that we looked at in Chapter 12, then you will realise that doing this should mean that you will have resolved *some* of the problems. If you have brought your hero and heroine to some sort of an understanding, resolved or at least smoothed out some of the conflict you've been dealing with, then you will have prepared the way.

Your heroine and hero won't have to clear up absolutely everything that's gone wrong between them, but just parts of it – usually the worst parts if you've got that Black Moment right.

So list what has to be done:

▶ What has to be explained?

▶ What has to be apologised for? What has to be put right?

▶ What has been misunderstood?

▶ What secrets have to be revealed?

▶ What has happened that involves other people?

▶ What has to be proved and what proof will do this?

▶ What points will no longer need to be proved to the person who doubted before – because of their love – but will still have to be proved by the person who was doubted – because of their love?

▶ What do the hero and heroine need to put on one side so that they can go forward happily and confidently into the future?

▶ And what will give them the necessary *balance* so that there is no winner, no loser – only equals?

Then you write it. And you try to make it a rounded, satisfying and emotional read that will have your reader smiling in contentment, and wishing there was more of this great story, as she closes the book.

14

Practicalities

Once you have written your novel, you will try to get it published. In this chapter we will look at some of the important practical details you will need to consider.

Do you need an agent?

The world of publishing is a crowded and competitive one and so you need all the help you can get. There are many publishers who will not even look at any unsolicited material unless it comes to them from an agent.

But romance fiction tends to be a specialised field all of its own. There is *one* giant publisher – Harlequin Mills & Boon – with almost a monopoly on romance publishing, and the others are much smaller companies.

I have never had an agent in all the time I have been writing for Harlequin Mills & Boon. I know of other authors who have, but I don't know of any major differences or improvements that their agents have acquired for them. Certainly, Mills & Boon are more than happy to read any unsolicited manuscript and they don't specify that it needs to come from an agent.

Finding an agent can be as difficult – if not more – than finding a publisher, and many agents won't look at category or series fiction books. My advice would be to submit your work to the publisher in this case. If you are in the single title market or move into it, then that would be the time to look for an agent for your work.

If you want to find an agent, then there are a couple of valuable reference books to help you.

> *The Writer's Handbook* edited by Barry Turner (Macmillan)
> *The Writer's and Artist's Yearbook* (A&C Black)

Both are published annually and they list all the UK agents, together with details of the sorts of books that they are looking for and specialise in. Study these carefully and choose an agent who deals in popular fiction and romance or women's fiction.

Don't waste an agent's time – and yours – and your money by sending off queries to agents who don't handle fiction or specify that they don't want romance or any sort of genre fiction. Like everyone else in the publishing world, agents are very busy people and they probably won't even spare your work more than a glance before putting it back in the envelope and returning it to you.

Studying the market

The first thing you need to do before you submit your work to an editor is to study your market. We've looked at some ways to do this in the first chapter of this book, but when you are getting ready to submit you need to study the market carefully.

The two reference works I cited above will give you a lot of help. As well as agents, they list UK and international publishers giving details of the type of books they publish and the type of submissions they prefer.

Obviously, in the romance field, Harlequin Mills & Boon and their Silhouette lines is the publisher whose name immediately springs to mind when looking for somewhere to send your short series romance. But there are other romance publishers you might want to consider, particularly if your book is not strictly a series or category romance.

Some of these are:

► Avalon Books
► Avon Books/HarperCollins
► Dorchester Publishing
► Kensington
► Penguin Putnam Inc
► Random House Inc
► St Martin's Press
► Simon and Schuster
► Warner Books

If you feel you need an agent, study the details given in the reference books, and make sure you only send them the type of book that they are asking for. This may sound so basically obvious that it doesn't need to be said, but there are plenty of publishers – Harlequin Mills & Boon included – who have been sent totally inappropriate manuscripts that they would never publish. Once again, don't waste an editor's time and your money in posting off something that they don't want.

Studying publisher's guidelines

When you have decided on a publisher, make sure that you study their guidelines to confirm that your book is appropriate for their house, and particularly for the line you want to aim for.

Harlequin Mills & Boon provide detailed guidelines for each line that they publish. You will find these on their websites – the web addresses for these are in the Reference and Resources section at the end of this book. Check out the 'Learn to Write' sections on each site and read the guidelines for each imprint.

Preparing your work for submission

You've decided to bite the bullet and send your novel straight to a publisher. First of all, you need to make sure that your manuscript is professionally prepared and presented. These are the basic things you need to remember:

▶ Make sure that your manuscript is typed or word-processed as clearly and as cleanly as possible. Don't use a fading ribbon that leaves only a pale grey script. It needs to be as easy to read as you can make it.

▶ Use plain white, good quality A4 paper. Again this might seem obvious, but my own editor has had submissions on dark red paper.

▶ Margins should be at least 25mm (1 inch) wide on all sides. If you're lucky, an editor may write some helpful comments on your manuscript and you need to make sure that she has space to do so.

▶ Only print on one side of the paper.

▶ Do not staple or bind the manuscript in any way.

▶ Double space the lines.

▶ Use a readable font in a reasonable size, for example Times New Roman, Courier or, Courier New in 12 point type. Don't use fancy script styles – that dark red submission referred to above was printed in italic script!

▶ Always remember that an editor has a lot of manuscripts to read. It's only courteous and considerate to make her job as easy as possible. Putting an editor in a bad mood just as soon as she sees your typescript is *not* a good idea.

▶ Number your pages consistently throughout, putting them in the same place – usually the centre of the bottom line of the page.

▶ Use a header at the top of every page except the title page. Your header should include your book's title and your name.

▶ The title page should show the title of the book, the author's name, the approximate number of words and be centred on the page. Add your real name (if you write under a pen name) and full address at the lower right of the title page.

The word count

Series romances have very specific word counts – usually around 50,000–55,000 words. The details for the line you are targeting will be given in the guidelines available. The word counts are there for a reason. Series books are produced to a standard format, with the same size of book and the same number of pages in each volume.

But the fact that they have exactly the same number of pages does not always mean that they have the exact same number of words in them. The size of the print and the size of the margins surrounding it can be altered to some extent so that the book fits into the right number of pages. But if there are too few words then the font will be too big and the book will look like a Janet and John reader. Too many words and the print will be too small to read comfortably.

That 55,000 word limit (or whatever it is for the line you've chosen) has been deliberately selected to make the book look as good and be as readable as possible, so do try to keep within it. But don't panic and worry yourself into a frenzy if your word count is not spot on. A good editor is probably going to be able to find plenty of places in the book where you need to 'cut for pace', and so reduce the word count if necessary.

What you need to do is to make sure that you have come as close to the limit as possible, making sure that you have as little padding or repetition as you can. Then if you still can't prune your work any more, wait to hear what an editor has to say.

Remember, a book that's too short is not a good idea either. Again that word count has been calculated to give the reader a satisfactory reading experience. Too short a book will short-change her on some part of that experience and she won't enjoy it as much as she could. Writing tightly and with pace is a great idea – but not at the expense of only giving the reader half a book.

How to calculate a word count

Word counts are awkward things. Some publishers work on the word count that your computer uses, which makes life easy. You click on the right button on your computer and the work is done for you. This is usually acceptable for the UK editorial department of Harlequin Mills & Boon – the lines that are edited in Richmond, Surrey.

But the American lines and editors work rather differently. They calculate word counts in quite another way, and they can be particular about just what the count is. So you need to know what they want and provide it.

This is the information on the way that word counts are calculated for a USA submission:

▶ It's not *really* word count. It is the translation of page count into an assumed number of words per page. So, if you used the actual word count, instead of page count, you would end up with more than 10,000 words. This is too many which would mean you would have to cut a lot of your work.

▶ Each line of words is *assumed* to be 10 words, no matter how many you actually use. It's allotted space. Use it all, use less, use more, it doesn't matter. It's assumed to be 10 words.

▶ No matter what kind of computer program you use, you should be able to average out close to 250 words a page.

▶ These are the settings for either PCs or Macs to average 25 lines to a page and so get close to the 250 words to a page:
  – 1 inch margins all around.
  – Courier or Courier New 12, Times New Roman 14 fonts. They are also *known* to yield the average you are looking for.
  – Include a header, left justified. First line – title, second line – *your* name, tab over until one tab from right corner, insert page number, third line – blank.
  How to calculate publishers' word count:
  250 (the allotted number of words) × number of pages = publishers' word count.
  For example: **250 words × 340 pages = 85,000 words.**

Submitting your work to an editor

Only send what they ask for!

Different publishing houses have different requirements for submissions. You should always find out exactly what is wanted for the publisher and the particular line that you are aiming at. Here again, those reference books will come in handy, and so will the information on the websites.

If you check the Mills & Boon website and then the Harlequin one, you will immediately see an important difference in what an editor wants to see as part of your first submission.

North American submissions

The offices in New York and Toronto do not accept unsolicited complete or partial manuscripts, but ask instead that you submit a query letter. The query letter should include a word count and pertinent facts about yourself as a writer, including your familiarity with the romance genre. You should indicate what series you think your project is appropriate for, if it is completed, what you think makes it special, and previous publishing experience (if any). Also include a synopsis of your story that gives a clear idea of both your plot and characters and is no more than two single-spaced pages. A self-addressed envelope and return international postage coupons will ensure a reply.

UK submissions

The UK offices of Harlequin Mills & Boon ask for something slightly different. They will look at a 'partial' manuscript – three chapters of your story. This is so that they can get an idea of your writing style and the way that you have started your story.

This is another of those seemingly obvious points – send the *first three chapters*! An editor wants to see how the story develops over the *first* chapters. They want to see if it is logical, punchy, moves at a pace that will grab the reader and if you have started to develop your characters within those chapters. But there have been authors who have selected three chapters from different points in the manuscript thinking that the editors want to see a selection.

You should also include a synopsis of your story and a covering letter. When you send in three chapters you should receive a confirmation letter (with a reference number) within two weeks (depending on where you live). If you don't receive a confirmation letter then call the office – as it means that your submission hasn't reached the office.

Sending a query letter

What should you put in a query letter?

If the letter is going to a UK office, along with a partial manuscript and a synopsis, then it is of less importance than one that is sent to an American office with just a synopsis for the editor to judge you by.

The problem with a query letter is to strike a balance between wanting to win an editor's interest and being businesslike. So you should always consider the following.

▶ Present it professionally – don't use scented notepaper, wild colours or cartoons.

▶ Word-process or type it – make it as readable as possible.

▶ Include the details asked for about any publishing success you have already had. You want to make yourself look appealing without showing off.

▶ Mention if you are a member of any professional associations (for example, the Romantic Novelists' Association or Romance Writers of America, etc).

▶ Think about the tone of the letter – you have to be confident without bragging, businesslike and yet creative.

▶ Tell the editor why you have aimed at this particular line, and what you think is original, special and interesting about your book.

▶ Try to get across something of the tone of the book you're hoping to submit – a touch of humour or a hint of intense emotion, or perhaps of suspense.

▶ Let the editor know whether the book is complete or not – this will give her some idea of whether she might have to wait to see the whole manuscript.

Sending a synopsis

What exactly is a synopsis? I've given you an example of a synopsis I wrote for my book *Constantine's Revenge* (see Chapter 11) so that you will have some idea of what is needed. But I dislike writing them and I'm quite convinced that I would never have sold my first book if I had tried to sell it with a query letter and a synopsis.

The synopsis is a summary of the plot of your novel. It encapsulates the story from start to finish, either chapter by chapter or in a narrative form like the example I have given. The length can range from a one page summary to a detailed synopsis that is almost a short story in itself. Harlequin Mills & Boon usually looks for a short, one-page synopsis at the start. The American offices are usually looking for a synopsis of about three pages. They want to see how the plot develops, the conflict that you have set up, what the characters are like, if there are any unusual twists to the story, and how you resolve the conflict in the end.

As I say, I am no expert on writing synopses but these are the suggestions I would make:

▶ Make sure you tell the larger outline of your story clearly and concisely. Don't get bogged down in minor details of the heroine's job, the hero's family, etc.

▶ Concentrate on your hero and heroine, their developing relationship and the conflict that comes between them.

▶ Try to write the synopsis in the same sort of tone as the novel you've written – dark and intense or light and amusing. Don't make it flippant when the book is the exact opposite.

▶ Keep it as dramatic and engaging as possible.

▶ The only way I can write a synopsis reasonably well is to approach it as a mini short story. I try to write the story of my characters in condensed form but not just a list of 'He does this and she does that...'. That is why, in the examples I've given, I've included the one (Synopsis 2) that gives the details of *why* things happen.

▶ Finally, the point of a synopsis is to help the editor see how the story develops from the point of the three chapters she has read, so concentrate on that. Make sure that you include any original twists and turns, anything that you feel makes your story special and different. Remember, an editor sees so many manuscripts – Mills & Boon receive thousands of unsolicited submissions every year. So this is your opportunity to sell yourself and your novel.

▶ If you only get a chance to send a query letter and a synopsis then both of these are your only chance to demonstrate your writing skills – use them to the best advantage you can.

A submission checklist – what to include with your manuscript

This is a checklist for a partial submission of the sort that you should make to Harlequin Mills & Boon in London. If you are asked to submit a partial manuscript to any American office, then this will also apply.
  You should submit:

▶ The **first three** chapters of your manuscript.

▶ A **title page** giving the title, your name (or writing name if used), the approximate word count and below this, to the right of the page, your name, address and telephone number.

▶ A **covering letter** – keep it to a single page, but do tell the editor about any publishing experience you have had – short stories or articles accepted, for example. Also make sure that you say which line your novel is aimed at.

▶ A **synopsis** of your book.

▶ A **self addressed, stamped envelope** (commonly abbreviated to a SASE). This should be big enough to hold your submission – either partial or full manuscript – if the editor returns it to you as a rejection. Make sure you enclose enough postage for the full weight of the manuscript.
  If you are submitting to an American office, or if you live outside the country you are sending it to, then you should include international postage coupons for the correct amount, or a money order sufficient for the cost of postage. You should also include sufficient postage for the next item.

▶ **A notification postcard**. If you want to check that your manuscript arrived, it is a good idea to include a plain white postcard, stamped if possible, and addressed to you, much like the SASE. On the blank side, write something simple like 'Manuscript received on...date' so that the editor can sign it and drop it in the mail to let you know.

▶ An alternative to the points above, is that if you don't want to go to the trouble of buying and including postage and SASE, you can put a note in with your manuscript asking the editor to shred it rather than return it. In this case, the inclusion of a postcard so that the editor can let you know your manuscript hasn't been accepted and has been shredded will be vital.

Other important points

▶ Address the submission correctly – check the most recent address, on the website if possible. The reference books are often prepared six months or more in advance and are not always totally up to date.

▶ Always say which series you are aiming for – many editors deal with submissions for different lines.

▶ Address your letter and submission to the senior editor for the line you are aiming at. Your manuscript probably won't get read by him or her, by a junior editor, yet this is the most polite approach.

What happens next?

So you've submitted your partial – what do you now? I'm afraid that the painful truth is *you wait*. Things don't happen quickly in publishing and although Mills & Boon editors are as efficient as they can be – often amazingly so, considering the number of manuscripts they receive, they will often take several weeks to get round to reading your manuscript.

All unsolicited manuscripts that arrive on one day are passed on to the duty editor for that day. But that editor will also have contracted authors working with her, and this work must take priority so that the books are acquired by the scheduled date. There will also be authors whose partial has been read and the full manuscript asked for.

So please be patient. If you have received an acknowledgement of your submission's arrival, then sit tight, chew your fingernails and wait. The editor will get back to you as soon as she can. But the current estimate within which they hope to let you know is 16 weeks. For some of the American offices, the waiting time can be much longer.

The best thing to do is to get started on something else and concentrate hard. It isn't uncommon for some authors to send in a partial manuscript for a book they haven't even finished yet, so if you're in this situation you should get on and complete it. Brooding about the story you have submitted is not going to speed its assessment.

What is an editor looking for?

If you were to submit a novel to an editor, in the hope of publication, what she would be looking for would be:

▶ Lively characters, with an individual twist to them.

▶ A 'pace' to the novel that keeps it moving swiftly from one scene to the next, not slowing and losing the reader at any time.

▶ An emotional drive that would give the story that essential PTQ which means the reader cares for the characters and wants them to 'live happily ever after'.

▶ An individual 'voice' that meant the author was telling the story in her own way and not just as a copy of everything that has gone before.

▶ Your novel should show *above all else* that you have read some of the current output by the publisher you are aiming at, Harlequin Mills & Boon.

Good news or bad news?

Once an editor has read your work, she will let you know her opinion. There are several possible outcomes:

▶ A rejection.
▶ A rejection with some detailed information about why this submission didn't work.
▶ A request for revisions on the partial.
▶ A request for a full manuscript.

If you get a rejection – feel free to admit that it hurts! This is a part of the world of the professional writer that no author *ever* gets used to. And believe me, even when you are an accepted, even a published author, it can still happen. So start learning your survival strategies now. Shout, stamp your feet, cry, throw the manuscript at the wall.

But also remember that a rejection is almost like a badge of honour. It is your first evidence that you are serious about trying to become a writer. Every published author has had them – maybe more than they care to remember. And although you might feel now that you will never, ever, put yourself through this again – also remember that even if submitting feels like sending your baby out into the wide world alone and unprotected, it is also the only way you ever will be published. No book was ever picked up from the author's desk at home. If you submit, you risk rejection, but if you never submit, you will never be accepted.

Apart from the straight rejection, any one of these responses should make you study carefully the letter you've been sent. You might not feel like it right at this moment, but editors are so busy that if he or she has taken the time to write a comment or two it means that he or she felt your work deserved it.

Dealing with revisions

It doesn't matter whether you are asked for revisions at the partial or at the full manuscript stage – the revision letter can be a daunting experience. You sent off what you thought was a good submission – the best you could write – and now someone has ripped it to pieces (it will seem that way) and wants you to completely rework it. (Probably it's not as bad as that but it feels like it!)

Read that letter and then read it again. If necessary put it away for a while and come back to it later when you feel calmer and your head is clearer.

Don't touch your manuscript until you've had time to think, to make sure you really understand what the editor is asking for, and hopefully *why*. Then when you feel ready, and in control of the situation, do your best to implement the changes suggested.

The important thing to remember at this stage is that the editor is on your side and would like to see your manuscript as a book that she or he can buy. That is their job – looking for books to publish. So you and the editor will *work as a team* to try to make your book the best it can possibly be – hopefully to make it publishable.

But always remember that this is not an automatic progression from working on revisions. No matter how hard you work, no matter how well you think you have followed the editor's suggestions, it is still, sadly, perfectly possible for the reworked manuscript not to come up to scratch.

The reasons why a manuscript doesn't work even after revisions can be many.

You may have rewritten that book too many times, revised it too much by then so that you've written all the spark, the freshness, out of it. That's one of the most common reasons why a revised book can fail.

Another is that a writer deals with the revisions in a 'corrections' way and doesn't incorporate them fully into the story. Or they can put the revisions in without really getting into the spirit of why they're needed.

Too often a writer will rush at the revisions to get them done and the manuscript returned to the publisher, but they haven't thought about what the editor asked them to do.

Sometimes, sadly, it's just a fact that the revisions suggested – and they are usually only suggestions – don't actually work. The editor tried, the writer tried, but really this story was never going to be quite right.

However, the revising experience is never wasted. You can always learn a lot from it about how to put a book together and how to shape it to the particular market involved. It also helps the editor see if you can work to revisions or even if you're willing to try. Unfortunately, there are writers who say 'No, my ms is perfect! I'm not changing a word. If you don't want it someone else will.'

Working on revisions, even if they don't work, is another step forwards, a toe in the door. The editor will remember you and know you are co-operative and prepared to work on revisions. Hopefully you'll get another chance with your next submission.

And let me let you into a secret. I can speak on this with feeling. Early in my career, a long time ago, I once wrote a book called *Chase the Dawn*. I *couldn't* get that one right. *Three* rewrites later, when all the freshness had gone from it, my editor suggested we leave it. I put it away and tried to forget about it. But I wanted to tell that story. So a couple of years later I pulled it out again. I read it through – and suddenly saw just where I'd been going wrong all the time. I rewrote it *again* and it was finally accepted.

So, even published authors get books rejected after revisions. It is important to see this experience as progress and learning, and to keep trying. But get used to revisions, as they're likely to be a fact of your life from now on, if you get accepted.

Different types of revisions
I'm often asked what sort of revisions editors suggest, so here is just a selection of what you might be asked for.

► To correct faults of logic, possibility, timing, chronology – anything that is not right in the actual factual telling of your story.

► To make your characters more realistic/believable/sympathetic.

► Usually allied with this – to deepen and strengthen their motivations (that question *why?* again).

► To add more dialogue.

► To tighten the pace so that the book reads more quickly. This usually involves that phrase 'cut for pace'.

► To deal with the sagging middle.

► To change the events of a plot that doesn't work in the hope of making it succeed.

► To make certain points clearer.

► To reduce flashbacks and keep more of the book in the present.

► And of course, the most common and frequently repeated problem is that the book 'lacks emotional punch'.

Getting another opinion

If you haven't had any feedback from the editor you sent your submission to, or if you would prefer to have someone look at it before you actually send it to a publisher, there are ways of getting a critique of your work. Most of these you will have to pay for.

Harlequin run their own critique service, the details of which are on their American website. The romance writing experts at *eHarlequin.com* will review and assess your story and offer detailed editorial advice.

One of the best suggestions I can make is that you join the Romantic Novelists' Association (RNA). The address is in the reference section at the back of this book.

RNA New Writers' Scheme

The RNA not only offers support and encouragement to both published and non-published authors, but it runs an excellent New Writers' Scheme. The cost of entry to this scheme is included in the subscription that a new writer (i.e. an unpublished writer) pays to join the Association.

Under this scheme, the new writer submits a typescript of a full-length novel for appraisal. These scripts are accepted at any time up to the end of September. Guidance is given beforehand on basic matters such as presentation, which help to give a professional appearance.

The organiser has a team of over 30 readers, mostly authors with extensive publishing histories in every type of romantic novel, or experienced editors.

The scripts are sent to an appropriate reader who understands the market the book is aimed at, and the reader provides a comprehensive report covering such aspects as suitability for that market, plotting, characterisation, pace, dialogue, style, and many more. These reports are honest – they point out faults and do not attempt to flatter, but they are also constructive in indicating where writers need to concentrate their efforts if they want to succeed.

About 10% of the scripts submitted which are considered ready, or almost ready, for publication are sent to another reader, and some of these are submitted to publishers by the RNA. The Association cannot act as an agent, but publishers and agents look at their recommendations carefully, and if they cannot take that script often make suggestions for further improvement. These scripts, and others, after revision, often find publishers.

As well as entry into the New Writers' Scheme, your subscription to the RNA will give you admission to the regular meetings, copies of the RNA NEWS, and a chance to attend the annual conference.

Romance Writers of America

In America, the RWA is the major association for romance writers. Their monthly *Romance Writers' Report* is full of articles on writing, information on publishers and details of the many contests that unpublished authors can enter in America. Many of these contests offer some feedback to authors who have entered them.

The largest and most prestigious of these is the Golden Heart Award which is presented annually at the RWA National Conference in July each year at the same ceremony at which the RITAs – the major prizes for the best of published romances – are awarded.

Receiving an acceptance

What happens if the revisions work and the editor wants your book?

First the manuscript has to be seen by several more people – a senior editor for the line, the editorial director. It will be taken to an acquisition meeting and finally you will get 'the call'.

The editor will phone you and tell you that she or he wants to buy your book. Editors enjoy this moment almost as much as the new author they are speaking to.

At this point congratulations are very definitely in order. Celebrate. Open the champagne. Tell everyone. You deserve it. Only a small percentage of the thousands of submissions that are sent to the romance publishing houses ever make it into the bookshops. So if you get an acceptance you've really achieved something.

Soon you'll be sent a contract – it's a standard one for all authors, but read it carefully and don't be afraid to ask if there is any part of it you don't understand. This is a whole new world, no one expects you to know everything.

Meeting deadlines

As a contracted author, you'll be asked to agree to writing a number of books each year. The dates that these completed manuscripts are to be delivered by will be included in your contract. However enthusiastic you feel, and however keen you are to launch your new career as a published author, try to be sensible about this. Don't take on more than you can manage comfortably. Once you're dealing with deadlines and delivery dates you will lose some of the freedom and fun of being a non-published author. Those deadlines are fixed, so you can't wait around for inspiration, only writing when an idea strikes.

You will need to be disciplined, businesslike and professional. Once the excitement of your acceptance has sunk in and faded a little, it can be another year or so before you actually see the book in your hand. But when you do it will be a thrill – a moment to treasure and to remember.

But don't think you've left the world of nervous worry about your submissions and the slog of revisions behind for ever. For the professional writer as well as for the amateur, such things are a way of life.

And finally...

So that's it. We've covered all the 12 points, discussed why they're important and thought about how they're used in the books you've read. I hope you've tried at least some of the writing exercises to see how it works in practice.

And what I hope you've learned is that to write a book with that all-important Page Turning Quality you need to:

▶ **Focus** on the **hero and heroine.**

▶ Create an intense **conflict.**

▶ Let your **plot** develop from your characters.

▶ Add plenty of **dialogue.**

▶ Use that **vital vulnerability** to create and build the **emotion** you know the readers like.

▶ Put in touches of **sensuality**, stir in some special **passion.**

▶ Keep asking yourself (and your characters) the question **why?**

▶ When the **Black Moment** comes it should be deep and dark, apparently insoluble, but a well-written resolution will bring you, your characters and your reader to a **believable happy ending.**

Thanks for sharing this book. I hope you've enjoyed it as much as I have. I wish you every success with your own writing.

Further Reading and Reference

Books

Books on writing skills
Donna Baker, *Writing A Romantic Novel and Getting Published*, Teach Yourself Books (Hodder & Stoughton: 1997)

Julie Beard, *The Complete Idiot's Guide To Getting Your Romance Published* (Alpha Books: 2000)

Emma Darcy, *The Secrets of Successful Romance Writing* (Random House: 1995)

Vanessa Grant, *Writing Romance* (Self-Counsel Press: 1997)

Yvonne MacManus, *You Can Write a Romance* (Coronet Books: 1983)

Leigh Michaels, *Writing the Romance Novel* (PBL Limited: 1999)

Marina Oliver, *Writing Romantic Fiction: How to make a success of your creative work* (How To Books Ltd: 1997)

Valerie Parv, *The Art of Romance Writing* (Allen & Unwin: 1993)

Jean Saunders, *The Craft of Writing Romance* (Allison & Busby: 1995)

Kate Walker, *A Straightforward Guide to Writing Romantic Fiction* (Straightforward Publishing: 2002)

Mary Wibberley, *To Writers With Love* (Buchan & Enright: 1987)

Books on the Romance Genre
Jay Dixon, *The Romance Fiction of Mills & Boon 1909–1990s* (UCL Press: 1999)

Jayne Ann Krentz, *Dangerous Men and Adventurous Women: Romance Writers on the Appeal of the Romance* (University of Pennsylvania Press: 1992)

Joseph McAleer, *Passion's Fortune: The Story of Mills & Boon* (Oxford University Press: 1999)

Journals

Romance Writers' Report (monthly) the journal of Romance Writers of America.

Romantic Novelists' Association News (quarterly) the journal of the Romantic Novelists' Association UK.

Romantic Times – American monthly magazine of reviews and articles on Romance.

Organisations

Romance Writers of America 16000, Stuebner Airline Road, Suite 140, Spring, Texas 77379 USA

Romantic Novelists' Association RNA Hon Membership Secretary, 38 Stanhope Road, Reading, Berkshire RG2 7HN

Romance Writers of Australia RWA Inc. PO Box 37, Somerton, Victoria 3062 Australia

Romance Writers of New Zealand RWNZ, P.O. Box 64–311 Botany Town Centre, Manukau City, New Zealand

Websites

www.cataromance.com
A site with lots of interest for readers and writers of Category Romance. It has articles on American, UK and Australian books and authors, reviews, etc.

www.eharlequin.com
Harlequin's main North America website, with details of authors and their books, plus extras like writing guidelines and message boards.

www.harlequinromanceauthors.com
The site for Harlequin Romance and Mills & Boon Tender Romance authors.

www.harlequin.presents.com
The site for Harlequin Presents and Mills & Boon Modern Romance authors.

www.kate-walker.com
Kate Walker's website.

www.harlequinmedicalwriters.com
The Harlequin and Mills & Boon Medical Writers website.

www.millsandboon.co.uk
The UK site for Harlequin Mills & Boon. Guidelines and submission details are available here.

www.romanceaustralia.com
Romance Writers of Australia.

www.romancewriters.co.nz
Romance Writers of New Zealand.

www.romantictimes.com
The website of *Romantic Times* magazine.

www.rna-uk.org
UK Romantic Novelists' Association website.

www.rwanational.org
Romance Writers of America.

Romance novels referred to in this book
All published by Harlequin Mills & Boon

Lynne Graham	*Prisoner of Passion* Mills & Boon *Presents*1996	
Joanna Maitland	*Marrying the Major* Historical Romance 2002	
Anne McAllister	*The Inconvenient Bride* Modern Romance 2001	
Michelle Reid	*Gold Ring of Betrayal* Mills & Boon *Presents* 1996	
	The Sheikh's Chosen Wife Modern Romance 2002	
Kate Walker	*A Sicilian Husband* Modern Romance 2003	
	Chase The Dawn 1988*	
	Constantine's Revenge Mills & Boon *Presents* 2000	
	Fiancée By Mistake Mills & Boon *Presents* 1998	
	Game of Hazard 1986*	
	His Miracle Baby Modern Romance 2001	
	Man of Shadows 1987*	
	The Groom's Revenge Mills & Boon *Presents* 1997	
	The Hired Husband Mills & Boon *Presents* 1999	
	The Hostage Bride Modern Romance 2001	
	The Sicilian's Wife Modern Romance 2002	
	The Unexpected Child Mills & Boon *Presents* 1997	
	Their Secret Baby Modern Romance 2004	

*These books were published before the Mills & Boon lines were split into two

Kate Walker's Protégé Programme

Kate Walker wants to help you

Kate Walker is committed to helping new writers in the Romance genre. She has been highly successful and sells millions of books because of the quality of her story telling but also because of the help she was given when she started writing. Now she believes it is her turn to help new writers and that is why she has written this book.

Kate now spends much of her time teaching on writing courses and is a regular at many of the Writer's Holidays, including the highly successful Writer's Holiday in Caerleon, South Wales, UK.

Now Kate Walker has made a commitment to help you. Kate has agreed to write more books in the future to help you to become a more accomplished writer. She is currently planning new books that examine other areas of romance writing and how to help new writers like you to become more professional and change your life to become an established and published writer.

If you wish to hear about future books and other goods from Kate Walker, to help you to become a professional writer, please photocopy this page, fill in your details and return it to:

Kate Walker's Protégé Programme
Studymates Publishing Limited
PO Box 2
Bishops Lydeard
Somerset TA4 3YE

Yes please send me information about future Kate Walker books and other goods. I understand that by sending in this form, I am not obliged to make any purchase. I further understand that Studymates Publishing will NOT pass on my details to any third party and that my statutory rights under English Law are safeguarded.

Name_____

Address_____

_____

_____

Post Code_____Phone Number_____Date_____

Email_____Signature_____

Index